Health and healing figure prominently in the New Testament gospels, which portray Jesus confronting a variety of sicknesses, from paralysis to blindness, and epilepsy to abnormal behaviour. Did Jesus really heal those afflicted with these various maladies? Why did the sick come to Jesus? Were there no physicians? Had physicians failed them? Could they not afford to pay them?

This book sets the ancient reports of Jesus as healer in the context of the ancient world of "home remedies," medicine, physicians, and healers. It compares him with other healers of the day and shows how each of the four New Testament gospels offers distinctive portraits of Jesus as healer. We see him as one of many healers in his day, but yet set apart as a "wounded healer" – powerful yet in the end powerless, and thus achieving the ultimate "healing," victory over death. The book follows the reputation of Jesus as healer into the "apocryphal" Christian writings and into the stories of Jesus healing through his followers. Drawing on recent scholarship on Jesus and on sociological, anthropological, and medical studies of sickness and healing, the author offers a carefully weighted response to the question, "Did Jesus really heal?" The Questions for further thought and discussion and the Suggestions for further reading at the end of the volume provide readers with opportunity for further exploration of questions raised in the book.

Understanding Jesus Today

JESUS AS HEALER

Understanding Jesus Today

Edited by Howard Clark Kee

Growing interest in the historical Jesus can be frustrated by diverse and conflicting claims about what he said and did. This series brings together in accessible form the conclusions of an international team of distinguished scholars regarding various important aspects of Jesus' teaching. All of the authors have extensively analyzed the biblical and contextual evidence about who Jesus was and what he taught, and they summarize their findings here in easily readable and stimulating discussions. Each book includes an appendix of questions for further thought and recommendations for further reading on the topic covered.

Other books in the series

Howard Clark Kee, *What Can We Know About Jesus?*
Pheme Perkins, *Jesus as Teacher*
David Tiede, *Jesus and the Future*
John Riches, *The World of Jesus: First-Century Judaism in Crisis*
James D. G. Dunn, *Jesus' Call to Discipleship*
Victor Paul Furnish, *Jesus According to Paul*

Jesus as Healer

HAROLD REMUS

Department of Religion and Culture, Wilfrid Laurier University

CAMBRIDGE
UNIVERSITY PRESS

Published by the Press Syndicate of the University of Cambridge
The Pitt Building, Trumpington Street, Cambridge CB2 1RP, United
Kingdom

CAMBRIDGE UNIVERSITY PRESS
The Edinburgh Building, Cambridge CB2 2RU, United Kingdom
40 West 20th Street, New York, NY 10011–4211, USA
10 Stamford Road, Oakleigh, Melbourne 3166, Australia

First published 1997

Printed in the United Kingdom at the University Press, Cambridge

A catalogue record for this book is available from the British Library

Library of Congress cataloguing in publication data

Remus, Harold, 1928–
Jesus as healer / Harold Remus.
        p.   cm – (Understanding Jesus today)
Includes bibliographical references and index.
ISBN 0 521 58469 8 (hardback) – ISBN 0 521 58574 0 (paperback)
1. Jesus Christ – Miracles.   2. Healing in the Bible.
I. Title.   II. Series.
BT366.R44   1997
232.9'55 – dc20   96-36260 CIP

ISBN 0 521 58469 8 hardback
ISBN 0 521 58574 0 paperback

Contents

Preface

In the pages that follow the symbols // are used to indicate parallel passages in the New Testament gospels, for example, Mark 2:13–17//Matt. 9:9–13, Luke 5:27–32. Unless otherwise noted, the scripture quotations are from the New Revised Standard Version of the Bible (copyright 1989 by the Division of Christian Education of the National Council of Churches of Christ in the USA) and are used by permission with all rights reserved. Translations of other ancient writings are my own.

Dates in the ancient world are indicated by "BCE" (Before the Common Era) and "CE" (Common Era), for example, 136 BCE and 30 CE.

I treat Mark as the first New Testament gospel, and the authors of Matthew and Luke as working from Mark, though not necessarily our version of Mark. Some scholars place Matthew first chronologically, with the author of Mark shortening Matthew to give us what we know as the Gospel of Mark, and the author of Luke employing both Matthew and Mark in composing the gospel of Luke. Regardless of theories of origin, the distinctive natures of each of these three gospels, as pointed out in chapters 2 through 4, remain.

The word "pagan," commonly used in a negative sense in current usage, I employ in a neutral sense to mean, simply, non-Jewish and non-Christian.

The "Suggestions for further reading" at the end of the book offer information on how to find the various ancient writings and modern studies referred to in the book; other titles that may prove helpful in pursuing a particular subject are also included. The "Questions for further thought and discussion" may prove helpful in reflecting on the various chapters of the book.

I want to thank my one-time teacher, Howard Clark Kee, for the invitation to write this book, which accords with various long-standing academic and personal interests of mine.

To Catherine Huggins, Administrative Assistant in the Department of Religion and Culture, Wilfrid Laurier University, Waterloo, Ontario, I owe a large debt of gratitude for translating my sometimes barely decipherable script into laser-print. My colleagues in the Department and in the Canadian Society of Biblical Studies are also owed my thanks for encouragement and inspiration over the years of what might be termed the gestation of this little volume.

My wife, Alice Croft, applied her usual painstaking editing and proofreading skills to the typescript and the index and her usual patience and understanding to her husband's psyche. Carolyn, my first wife, who knew about sickness and death and taught me much about both, was often in my thoughts as I wrote. Both have a share in what follows.

Chapter 1

Jesus as Healer: Prologue

By the fifth chapter of the Gospel of Mark Jesus' reputation as a healer is firmly established by the author. Amid throngs of people, he is sought out by the sick. In one such scene, a man named Jairus, a leader of a Jewish synagogue, approaches Jesus and begs him to come and heal his daughter (5:22–23).

On the way to Jairus' house, however, there is an interruption (5:25–34). A woman approaches Jesus from behind, touches his cloak, and is immediately healed of the hemorrhage that has long plagued her. Jesus, perceiving "that power had gone forth from him," stops and asks who touched his cloak, whereupon the woman comes forth and tells her story.

It is a story typical of many, not only in the ancient world but in our own day as well. For a dozen years the woman has consulted physicians about her problem, exhausting her financial resources in the process – all to no avail. In her desperation she turns, as do many in our day, to a person who would today probably be labeled a "faith healer." She has already likely exhausted what we today commonly call "home remedies" and "alternative medicine." One third of Americans, it is reported, turn to alternative medicine every year – this despite the annual expenditure of billions on conventional medicine in the health-care industry. Incurable, chronic illnesses account for much of this, especially of the sixty percent of those Americans over sixty-five who turn to "unproven therapies." But poverty, or the fear of being impoverished by conventional

1

medical treatment, as the woman was, also has something to do with this phenomenon.

The cost of health care today drives debates on the subject, not only in the United States, but in other countries as well. There is a crucial difference between the woman's world and ours, however. For a person laid low by sickness in her day there were no medical "safety nets," as there are in most of the so-called developed world today. Debilitating illness, or disability resulting from an accident while working, could mean descent into poverty and an untimely death. It was a world in which health was prized as the ultimate good. In the words of Aelius Aristides, a well-known orator who lived in the next century after Jesus, without health "one can neither make use of the good things of the soul nor enjoy any success whatever" (*Oration* 45.18). The modern equivalent is the television commercial that concludes, "If you've got your health, you've got just about everything." Aristides' own story of sickness makes clear that, while health was the highest good, people in his day did not bring to sickness the expectations we commonly have: that we will not *stay* sick; that a drug, an operation, a transplant will restore us to work and family. We are more apt to be surprised if we do *not* get well than if we do. Indeed, it has been suggested that one reason for the decline of institutional religion in the Western world is precisely this expectation: one has medical science, one doesn't need God.

For the hemorrhaging woman, and for Aristides, it was the reverse: restoration to health was iffy, expectations of recovery were low. Aristides' many ailments had led him to abandon his career. His story is both parallel to, and decidedly different from, the story of the woman in the Gospel of Mark. Together, however, they tell us much about the means people in the Greco-Roman world employed to deal with sickness and disability; their stories thus set the stage for seeing Jesus as healer in his own time.

Home remedies

The most common means of treating an ailment would be home remedies. Aristides does not mention any, but it is hardly possible that he, along with others in his day, would not have been acquainted with many such. They are known to us especially from ancient treatises on agriculture, which deal with the sicknesses not only of animals but also those of humans. In his *De Agri Cultura* (c. 160 BCE), for example, Cato, a farmer's son who rose to prominence in Rome, offers a recipe for laxative wines (secs. 114, 115), another for wine to retain urine (122) and to treat gout (123), and still others for various internal problems. His cure-all, however is cabbage (156–57). Cut up and taken internally, straight or in a mixture, raw or cooked, it would prevent indigestion, relieve bowel irritation, act as a purgative, and facilitate urination. Applied externally as a poultice and sterilizer, it would heal wounds, boils, fistulas, nasal polyps, and dislocations. Even washing a patient or a baby with the urine of a cabbage-eater would be medicinally beneficial, he says. In some cases, Cato recommends chanting to heal dislocations (140) – an indication of belief in the power of words, evident also in accounts of Jesus' healings (see chapter 2 below).

Readers of the Bible may recall similar remedies: the figs Isaiah instructs King Hezekiah's servants to apply to the king's deadly boil (2 Kings 20:1, 7); the draining and bandaging of bruises and sores and bleeding wounds (Isa. 1:6; cf. Luke 10:34); oil and wine applied to wounds or for healing generally (Isa. 1:6; Luke 10:34; Mark 6:13; James 5:14); the wine recommended for stomach trouble (1 Tim. 5:23). The dividing line between home or folk medicine and the medicine practiced by physicians was not so sharply drawn as it is today, however, and some of the treatments mentioned may have been recommended or employed by physicians.

Physicians and medicine in Jewish writings

Physicians are mentioned several times in the Bible. Those in Joseph's employ embalm his father Jacob (Gen. 50:2). King Asa turns to physicians, rather than to the Lord, to heal his feet (2 Chron. 16:12). Various folk sayings or proverbs assume that, when sick, one turns to a physician, presumably when home remedies fail (Jer. 8:22; Matt. 9:12//Luke 5:31). This is what the woman with the hemorrhage had likely done; so, too, Aelius Aristides. It is what the Roman writer Varro (116–27 BCE) recommends in his treatise on farming (*De Re Rustica* 1.16.4). The author of the Gospel of Mark tells us nothing about how the physicians treated the woman and what it was that she had suffered in their care. There was a considerable stock of medical lore devoted to women, notably the treatise *Gynae-cology* by the eminent Greek physician Soranus of Ephesus (98–138 CE), which influenced medicine down into the early modern period. There were also women physicians, medicine being one of the few professions open to women. Whatever the gender and credentials of the physicians consulted by the woman in the gospel account, treatment inappropriate to a woman, which a number of woman today have been protesting, may have contributed to what she had had to endure "under many physicians" (Mark 5:26).

Anything the Bible may say about the theory and practice of medicine has to be read from between the lines. However, Jewish writings current in Jesus' day and geographical area provide more information about physicians and medicines and other forms of healing then. *Sirach* (or *Ecclesiasticus*), the book of proverbs from around 180 BCE by the Jewish sage Jesus ben Sira ("Son of Sirach"), offers fulsome phrase of physicians for their skill, which (among other things) employs medicines prepared by pharmacists. All these – physicians, their skills and medicines, healing itself – are seen as gifts "from the Most

High" (*Sirach* 38.1–8). *Jubilees*, a writing from the mid-second century BCE, traces the Jews' knowledge of healing to a book written by Noah recording what angels had taught him about healing – "by means of herbs of the earth" – such illnesses as were caused by evil spirits (*Jubilees* 10.10.14). The Jewish historian Josephus, a near contemporary of Jesus born not long after Jesus' crucifixion, attributes directly to God the art of healing that wise King Solomon received to combat the diseases that demons inflict on humans; a charm said to have been composed by Solomon was used by a certain Eleazar, for example, to expel a demon in the presence of Vespasian, future emperor of Rome (*Antiquities* 8.45–46; see, further, chapter 2 below).

The Jewish War, Josephus' account of the Jewish revolt against Rome (66–73 CE), offers bits and pieces of information about medicines and physicians, and *Jewish Antiquities*, his lengthy retelling of the biblical history of Israel, embellishes the biblical accounts with details about medicine that he, along with other educated Jews, might have learned from Greek and Roman writers, or with which Jews generally might be expected to be familiar from their own experience. Josephus himself was the son of a midwife (*Life* 185), and through his involvement in the Jewish revolt he was acquainted first-hand with battle casualties and how they were treated. He mentions the medical help (Greek: *therapeia*) that the wounded received (*War* 1.246) and how three of his friends, taken down from the crosses on which they were crucified, received medical treatment, two of them in vain (*Life* 420–21). When King Herod is ill, he calls in his physicians (*Antiquities* 17.171), and in King Saul's illness Josephus assumes that the "servants" who in the biblical account advise Saul to seek someone to alleviate his mental state with music (1 Sam. 16:17) must have been physicians; however, the musician chosen – David – was, says Josephus, Saul's only (real) physician (*Antiquities* 6.166, 168).

Besides attending to the sick, reports Josephus, physicians perform useful deeds such as circumcision (*Antiquities* 20.46). On the other hand, sometimes, because of their knowledge of drugs, they might be implicated in plots to kill the sick (14.368). Similarly, Josephus reports that King Herod's brother died when he ate a dish to which had been added poison obtained from a woman from Arabia, such women surpassing all others, he says, in their knowledge of drugs (17.62–63). He ascribes somewhat similar lore to the Essenes, the Jewish sect commonly thought to have hidden the scrolls found in our time in caves on the west bank of the Dead Sea: they investigate roots and stones for possible healing properties (*Jewish War* 2.136).

Josephus mentions various symptoms and medical procedures: amputation of wounded or diseased limbs (*Jewish War* 1.507; 6.164–65) as well as inflammation (1.507), which can spread and infect all the members of the body (4.406–07) – a passage that recalls 1 Corinthians 12:26, where Paul speaks in similar fashion.

Like Paul, Josephus in these passages is speaking metaphorically. That both authors have recourse to the language of disease and medicine does not mean they had medical training any more than the use of medical terminology by the author of Luke–Acts meant he was a physician (as some scholars have maintained; see chapter 4 below). What it does indicate is that educated persons were apt to be acquainted with some of the language of medicine, even as they are today, and that such language would come readily to mind in a world where disease could quickly become life threatening and medical treatment was unpredictable. Moreover, as was mentioned earlier, the line between the professional practice of healing and healing as practiced day to day in households or on farms – "folk" medicine – was not sharply drawn.

Greek and Roman medicine

In his treatise on agriculture, Cato's authority for the medical recipes he dispenses is tradition and experience: they have been tested by time and will work. Only once does he offer a theory in explanation: veins gorged with food cause disease (*De Agri Cultura* 157.7). Theory is a basic element, however, in the seventy or so treatises ascribed to, or associated with, a Greek physician named Hippocrates (469–399 BCE) – a name familiar to modern people through the "Hippocratic Oath." Doctors today still profess its principles, if not the oath itself. The treatises themselves were consulted by physicians down to the rise of modern medicine in the nineteenth century. The Hippocratic doctrine of "humors" is reflected in our characterizing a person as being "in bad humor" or "out of humor." "Nature" – Greek *physis*, whence the term "physician" – also figures prominently in Hippocratic theory. "Nature" designated the normal human condition, that is, health, from which illness or injury was a departure and to which the physician sought to return the patient. The physician must take account of the nature of humans generally and of the patient individually as well as of the nature of the disease. Nature is itself a healing power, and the physician's art was modelled after nature.

Alongside theory, the Hippocratic treatises offer insights into the day-to-day world of physicians as well as the suffering of those who came to them for help. In terse case histories the author of *Epidemics*, for example, describes the progress of disease from first symptoms to recovery or to death. Unlike the New Testament gospels, where the ill are rarely named and their symptoms only vaguely described, the case histories often give the patients' names, where they lived, and detailed descriptions of their symptoms. The exceptions are predominantly women: seventeen of the eighteen women in the case studies go unnamed, like the hemorrhaging woman in the Gospel of Mark.

The descriptions, at the beginning of *Epidemics* 1, of the seasons in which the epidemics occurred imply that such information was important to the physician. The treatise *Airs, Waters, Places* goes further. From it we learn that, like itinerant healers such as Jesus, at least some Greek physicians travelled from place to place. On arriving in an unfamiliar city, the physician needed to take careful note, not only of the seasons, but also of the soil, water, air, in short the climate and environment (*Airs* 1); knowing these would give clues to what the local maladies were apt to be (2). The treatise provides some answers for various geographical areas. Thus, in a city with hot winds and brackish water the people will suffer from nasal and digestive disorders (3), whereas those in a cold climate will exhibit quite different symptoms (4). For the assertion that water from snow or ice is bad, the author offers experimental verification: measure some water into a container, put it outside in winter to freeze, bring it in to thaw, and observe the decrease in quantity, which the author attributes to the disappearance of the highest and best portion of the water (8).

More intriguing than this bit of theory is another assertion, namely, that all diseases are "divine" (*theia*) (22). This puzzling comment is illuminated by another Hippocratic treatise, *The Sacred Disease*. It is an attack on those who profess to heal, by what we today would call "religious" means, an affliction characterized by symptoms we associate with epilepsy (the word *epilepsis* occurs in section 13 of that treatise). The New Testament gospels report the healing of a boy with such symptoms (Mark 9:14–29//Matt. 17:14–21; Luke 9:37–43). For the gospel writers the affliction is anything but "sacred": it is caused by a "demon" or "an unclean spirit" that is possessing the boy, for which the appropriate treatment is to address the spirit and command it to depart (see chapter 2 below). Greek tradition labeled the disease "sacred" (*hierē*) or "divine" (*theion*) because of its extraordinary nature (*thaumasicn*) (*Sacred Disease* 1) and because it was thought a deity had possessed the person and could be identified from the way the person's behavior or speech resembled those associated with a particular deity (4). Those holding this view seek to treat the disease with purifications and incantations (2–4). For the author of the treatise this is a counsel of despair conceived by persons ignorant of its true causes; the author likens them to magicians, begging priests, and others whom he regards as charlatans (2). The disease is as "divine" as other diseases since it, like them, is caused by cold, sun, and winds – all of which are divine (*theia*) (21). Other diseases are no less extraordinary (1). The "sacred" disease can therefore be treated like any other disease by attending to its causes (which the author connects with the brain: 6–20) and the distinctive nature (*physis*) of the disease (1, 5, 21, 22).

Healers

The Hippocratic authors, and other medical writers such as Soranus of Ephesus mentioned earlier and the well-known physician Galen in the second century CE, were in possession of considerable medical lore belonging to their art. But when the physician's art failed, then the patient might turn to a healer: the hemorrhaging woman to Jesus, and Aelius Aristides to Asclepius, the Greek god whose healings Aristides describes as beyond medical art. Both Jesus and Asclepius, alone in the ancient world, came to be called simply "The Savior," and a rivalry developed between their followings. Aristides joined the poor and the rich (such as himself) who came to sleep in the Asclepius temple in Pergamum in Asia Minor (present-day Turkey) in hopes of receiving a dream or vision from the god that would bring them healing. Aristides describes in detail the afflictions he suffered and the relief he received. Aristides' physician shrewdly cooperated in the treatments the god prescribed, no matter how outlandish and contrary to medical practice and to ordinary common sense they appeared. Galen reported that he had himself become a follower of Asclepius after the god healed him of an abscess. At the Asclepius temple at Epidaurus in Greece the healings recorded in the inscriptions there could well be summarized in the evangelist's description of Jesus' healings (Matt. 4:23, 9:35) and those of his followers (10:1): "every disease and every sickness."

The healing stories at Epidaurus, in the gospels, and in other ancient sources conform to a basic pattern. One might have expected that the author of Mark would begin with the hemorrhaging woman's approach to Jesus and then conclude with the "whole story" she recounts when she is discovered (5:33). Instead the author begins with (1) a description of her sickness, so desperate that conventional means of healing have failed. Then comes (2) the approach to the healer, followed (3) by immediate cure, and (4) proof of the healing. Other details are included that add drama – Jesus asks who touched him and the disciples protest that he is surrounded by people touching him, the woman comes forward and tells all – but the basic form is clearly discernible, in this and other healing accounts of the times.

An example from the second-century CE is a story recounted by one of the characters in Lucian of Samasota's satire of credulous believers in miracle: (1) a farm worker is on the point of death after being bitten by a deadly viper; (2) a healer is called, who (3) uses a spell and a fragment from the tombstone of a young woman to work a healing, (4) evidence of which is seen in the man's picking up the pallet on which he has been carried and returning to work (*Lover of Lies* 11). Such stories were commonly told about persons like Jesus known for healing, but even when the person had no such reputation the basic pattern is still evident. Writing around the year 110 CE, the Roman historian Tacitus recounts a healing by the Roman general (and later emperor), Vespasian, in the year 60 CE: (1) two men, one blind, the other with a useless hand, both certified by physicians as incurable, (2) beseech Vespasian to heal them by moistening the blind man's cheeks and eyeballs with spit and by stepping on the useless hand which, after some persuasion, Vespasian does; (3) the healings follow, (4) as is attested to this day by witnesses (*Histories* 4.81).

Placed alongside accounts such as these and what is known of ancient medicine, Jesus as healer and the account of the healing of the hemorrhaging woman are seen to be not atypical. Persons hearing the Markan account of the hemorrhaging woman would recognize the form and identify with its elements: the sickness beyond medical art, Jesus as a type familiar to them in their world, the power that effects instant healing explicable only by reference to a power beyond that of humans. Such accounts would inspire hope, whereas the medical case histories mentioned earlier would make for depressing reading: of forty-two cases, almost two-thirds died. One is not apt, on the other hand, to hear of a healer's or a healing deity's failures. The New Testament account of the epileptic boy mentioned earlier reports that Jesus' disciples failed in their efforts to heal him; but that only makes Jesus' success in doing so all the more remarkable.

Early followers of Jesus were quick to assert, as have subsequent generations of Christians down to the present day, that Jesus was set apart from and superior to other healers of his day. More will be said of this in the next chapter. At the least, one must say that most other healers of the time were not known also as teachers, as Jesus was. But also, none ended their days powerless, hanging on a cross – a conclusion Jesus' first followers did not expect and with which they had to come to terms, as will be explained in subsequent chapters. These will treat Jesus as healer in each of the four New Testament gospels, for each gospel presents a distinctive portrait of him in that role. Then will come a chapter on Jesus as healer in early Christian sources outside the New Testament, another on Jesus as healing through his followers, and, finally, a chapter addressing the question whether Jesus really did heal.

Chapter 2

Jesus as Healer: The Gospel of Mark

The story of the healing of the hemorrhaging woman referred to
several times in the preceding chapter is presented in greatest
detail in the gospel thought by most scholars to be the first
written, the Gospel of Mark. Chronological priority is one
reason for beginning a study of Jesus as healer in early Christian
writings with the Gospel of Mark. Whether or not it was indeed
the first gospel (some scholars dispute that), there are other
factors that recommend it as a starting point: its brevity, per-
mitting a ready overview of the whole, and the fact that, in comparison with the other New Testament gospels, it devotes less
space to Jesus as teacher and more to what he does, including a
good number of healings. The author generally presents these in
more detail and more graphically than do the other evangelists.
Once one has some understanding of Jesus as healer in Mark,
then in subsequent chapters comparisons can more readily be
drawn with the other three New Testament gospels.

Jesus as healer

The healing stories, along with other miracle accounts, make
up much of the first nine chapters of the Gospel of Mark.
There emerges a Jesus who fulfills John the Baptist's proclamation that one mightier than he is yet to come (1:7): the
miracles signal that the reign of God that Jesus has announced
is near at hand (1:15). In the power of the Spirit that has
descended on him at his baptism (1:10), Jesus, through these
displays of power, demonstrates that God's reign is unfolding

13

He wondrously feeds multitudes of hungry people (6:30–44; 8:1–9), walks on water and stills wind and wave (6:45–51), and causes a fig tree to wither to its roots (11:14, 20–21). These wonders are outnumbered, however – indeed, overshadowed, one might say – by the many accounts of healings and expulsions of demons that occur in every one of the first ten chapters except chapter four, a collection of parables.

In several places the evangelist simply uses general terms or idioms to designate the many who come to Jesus for healing. They are "sick" (1:32, 34; 6:55, Greek, *kakōs echontas*, literally "being badly"; 6:56, *asthenountes*, literally "weak") or they have various "diseases" (*nosos* [1:34] and *mastix* [5:29, 34], both common terms for illness). In a number of passages, however, symptoms are reported. The mother-in-law of Simon (that is, Peter) is said to be in bed with a fever (1:30–31). A man disabled in some way by "paralysis" has to be carried on a pallet (2:3). A man has "a withered hand" (3:1); a woman has suffered for years with a discharge of blood (5:26, 29); a man is deaf and has trouble speaking (7:32); and two others are afflicted with blindness (8:22; 10:46).

Confronted with such symptoms, one school of Greek medicine, the Empiric, would likely have turned to treating them, applying remedies used successfully against such symptoms in the past without resort to much theory or diagnosis of the illness, even as today a health promotor in a Third World country who has been trained by a physician to recognize common problems may administer appropriate treatments without making an actual medical diagnosis. Physicians of another school of Greek medicine, the Dogmatists, would have wanted to pursue the causes of the symptoms, in order to make a diagnosis that would determine the treatment. They would doubtless have been frustrated by the evangelist's tersely rendered symptoms; for the purposes of a healing story, however, these laconic descriptions suffice.

Even the evangelist's labeling of a disease as "leprosy" would not have been very helpful to a Dogmatist physician, nor is it for modern readers. As the footnote to the New Revised Standard Version's rendering of Greek *lepros* as "leper", and *lepra* as "leprosy" (Mark 1:40, 42) states, these Greek terms "can refer to several diseases." That is, they do not necessarily denote what moderns call "leprosy" or "Hansen's disease," which the Greek medieval literature designated by the word *elephantiasis* (which, in turn, means something quite different today).

Persons with leprosy and the various symptoms noted above fall in the category of "sick" or "diseased" in Mark 1:32 and 34. Following these designations, however, is another that occurs frequently in the gospel and amounts to a diagnosis: persons exhibiting certain symptoms are said to be possessed by demons (1:32, 34; 6:13) or by "unclean spirits" (1:23, 26; 3:11; 6:7; 7:25). In a crucial passage in the gospel, Jesus is himself accused of "having" the ruler of demons, and is thus able to expel demons (3:22). Physicians adhering to the Hippocratic treatise *The Sacred Disease* discussed in chapter 1 above would likely have discounted any of these references to demons or unclean spirits and, after observing the symptoms, would prescribe medicines and diet appropriate to the disease.

That is not what happens in Mark or the other New Testament Gospels. Even though Jesus in Mark 2:17 refers to himself metaphorically and indirectly as a physician, and in the Gospel of Luke (4:23) applies to himself, ironically, a proverbial saying, "Doctor, cure yourself," he is not in fact a physician. Rather, people in his day, including readers of the gospels, would readily place him in another category suggested in chapter 1, that of healer. Whether that designation is adequate to the gospels' portrait of Jesus is an important question that will be addressed later on. Here it may be noted that various scholars, eager to distinguish Jesus from other miracle-workers and healers in his day, have argued that the very Greek words used by the gospel writers to designate the miracles they ascribe to him differ from those used by pagan writers reporting miracles worked by pagan miracle-workers. The evidence, however, does not support this claim. The gospel writers, along with other early Christian writers, the translators of the Hebrew Bible into Greek, and Jewish writers of the first century such as Philo and Josephus alike employ the same terminology as pagan writers.

Jesus and other healers

Similarly, some students of the New Testament have sought to distinguish between pagan and Christian accounts of healing on the basis of the behaviour of the healer: pagan healers and magicians (say these scholars) employed material means as well as various techniques, or "magical" formulas, whereas Jesus used only words; or the contexts of the healings in which Jesus is said to employ material means and technique allegedly set them apart from pagan healing accounts.

These are partial truths at best. In some instances, Jesus is indeed said to heal with words alone. "Be made clean [of your skin disease]!" (Mark 1:41). "I say to you, stand up, take your mat and go to your home" (2:11). "Stretch out your hand" (3:5). "Go; your faith has made you well" (10:52).

Rather than setting Jesus as a healer apart from pagans (and Jews) of his day, these utterances in fact situate him firmly in a world that was convinced of the power of words. The first book of the Bible begins with God's creating the world through utterances (Gen. 1), and the first verse of the Gospel of John asserts that "the word" was "in the beginning" (John 1:1). For ancient psalmists, God's word reigned over what God had created (Ps. 147:15–18; 148:8) and effected healing (Ps.

107:17–20). When Jesus identifies himself to those who come to take him prisoner by saying, "I am he," they fall to the ground at these words (John 18:5–6). Likewise, his powerful word commands illnesses, corpses, and demons, and they obey.

Similar demonstrations of the power of words are evident in sources outside the Bible, both Jewish and pagan. Rhythmic speech that would heal suffering was attributed to the ancient Greek philosopher Pythagoras (sixth century BCE) and to the legendary figure Orpheus (who appears, singing, in Christian catacomb art of the third century CE in Rome). About a thousand years after Pythagoras, a treatise from the collection of documents discovered at Nag Hammadi in Egypt in 1945 portrays a goddess as actually identifying herself with language (*Thunder: Perfect Mind* 6.14.10–15). In the so-called magical papyri from roughly the same time period and also discovered in Egypt, words are accorded power to influence cosmic forces; and the seven vowels of the Greek alphabet, when chanted, establish contact with the seven planetary deities (*Greek Magical Papyri* 4.605–30). As an antidote to a scorpion sting one is told to write certain characters on a piece of papyrus (the ancient form of paper), wrap it around the afflicted part, and the pain will disappear at once (7.193–96). A number of other such instructions for various ailments appear in subsequent lines of this particular papyrus (7.197–214). The Roman encyclopedist, Pliny the Elder (23/24–79 CE), notes that while the wisest persons reject this sort of belief in words and incantations, most people believe in them (*Natural History* 28.3.10), and the attention he devotes to them suggests that, deep down, he may have been one of them. The use of words in casting out demons will be considered later. None of this, one supposes, should surprise moderns ever since Freud and the advent of talk therapy, with the high hopes and expectations that are sometimes pinned on it.

Gestures and material means

Even as it is difficult to maintain that Jesus' use of words in
healing sets him apart from pagans and magicians, so too his
use of gestures and material means resemble those of other
ancient healers. In the healing of Peter's mother-in-law, Jesus
takes her by the hand and lifts her up (Mark 1:31). In healing a
leper, he touches him and commands that he be made clean
(1:41). In the healing of the deaf man who has trouble speaking,
a series of gestures and words is recounted. Jesus first takes the
man aside, then puts his fingers in the man's ears, spits, and
touches his tongue; he then looks upward, sighs, and says, "Be
opened." This command is recorded in Aramaic, *Ephphatha*,
and then translated into Greek (Mark 7:33–35). Aramaic, along
with a Greek translation, appears also in the account of Jesus'
raising a little girl from death. After he shoos away the
mourners, he takes her by the hand and commands her to get
up – *Talitha koum* (5:38–41). In healing the blind man of
Bethsaida he leads him out of the village, spits on his eyes, and
lays his hands on him (on his eyes?); the man recovers some
vision, but, as it is blurry, Jesus lays his hands on the man's
eyes (again?), whereupon he sees clearly (8:22–25).

None of these gestures and material means is unique to the
gospel accounts. Jesus' separating himself and the sufferer from
onlookers may remind one of how, today, doctor and patient
are customarily closeted together in a consulting room.
Though the patient knows that in conducting the examination
and making the diagnosis the doctor is calling on medical
science, for most patients that science is arcane – hidden from
them. The doctor's probing and thumping of the patient's body
is expected but yet somewhat mysterious; the doctor, too,
perhaps carries something of an aura of "otherness," a remote-
ness from the patient's everyday world symbolized by the
physician's white coat and stethoscope. Healers in Jesus' day

were not necessarily considered more than human (though the lines between divine and human were often not sharply drawn), but their powers and their arcane lore set them apart, and taking the sufferer apart from the public protected healers and their art from profanation and gave them scope to exercise it.

This is not an invariable motif either in the gospels or in other, contemporary sources, but it occurs frequently enough to warrant attention. Readers of the Bible may recall how Elijah (1 Kings 17:19) and Elisha (2 Kings 4:33) closet themselves with the boys they revive. In the *Metamorphoses*, a long work by the Roman poet Ovid (43 BCE–17 CE), Medea requires solitude to protect from profane eyes the arcane procedures she will use to rejuvenate an old man (7.255–57). The second-century philosopher and orator, Apuleius of Madaura in northern Africa (born c. 123 CE), on trial for his life for practicing magic, is accused of taking a boy and a few accomplices to a secret room and there casting spells on him (*Apology* 42). This accords with passages in the magical papyri that enjoin secrecy (*Greek Magical Papyri* 4.75) and sometimes specify a solitary place (3.616–17), with no one present (12.38). Healings by the deity Asclepius take place in Asclepius' temples, on holy ground set apart from the everyday. In the modern period, one may recall the folktale of the elves who stop making shoes for the impoverished shoemaker when they discover they are being spied upon.

Another feature sometimes found in healing accounts is the use of words in a language different from that of the narrative, such as the *Talitha koum* and the *Ephphatha* noted earlier. Such words are sprinkled throughout the magical papyri. They are also a stock element in the popular conception of healers. The pagan satirist, Lucian of Samosata (born c. 120 CE), includes the uttering of threats in Egyptian as part of the procedure he reports for driving out a spirit haunting a house

(*Lover of Lies* 31). Origen, the learned Alexandrian Christian author (*c*. 185—*c*. 254), explains that Egyptian names summon certain daemons, as do names in other languages; however, when translated into another tongue, they lose their power (*Contra Celsum* 1.24–25; 5.45). Similarly, spells effective in one language are ineffective in another, he says (1.25). For an early reader of the Gospel of Mark, it would make sense that the powerful words Jesus uttered in his native tongue, Aramaic, would be preserved in that language in the narrative. Early Christians engaged in healing rituals (see chapter 7 below) would also find it important to have available to them the very words Jesus spoke in healing, their efficacy undiluted by translation.

Jesus' use of saliva in healing is also not unique. Recall from chapter 1 Vespasian's healing of a blind man by applying saliva to his eyes. Pliny the Elder mentions the daily application of saliva as a remedy for eye diseases; indeed, not only does he regard saliva as effective in treating quite a number of ailments, he also reports on the usefulness of spitting in a variety of situations (*Natural History* 28.7).

Touch

Touch also plays an important role in ancient healing accounts (and is now enjoying a certain vogue in some current medical practice). Contact through the hand(s) is common, as in the healing of Peter's mother-in-law (Mark 1:31; cf. Acts 28:8) or the raising of a girl from death (Mark 5:41). It is what is sometimes requested of Jesus explicitly (Mark 5:23; 7:32), and presumably also when the request is simply for touching (8:22). In one of the Dead Sea scrolls, one means Abram uses to expel an evil spirit is the laying on of hands (*Genesis Apocryphon* 20.22, 28–29). Ovid tells the story of the legendary healer Aesculapius (the Latin spelling of Greek Asclepius), who revives a dead youth by touching his chest three times and speaking healing words three times (*Fasti* 6.753). Philostratus' *Life of Apollonius of Tyana* (c. 200 CE) depicts this first-century CE Neopythagorean sage and wonderworker as stopping the funeral procession of a young bride, touching her, and speaking inaudibly to her, whereupon she comes to life; Philostratus wonders whether she was really dead or still had some life in her and was warmed and revived by Apollonius' touch (*Life of Apollonius* 5.45). Presumably more warmth and vitality would come from full bodily contact, and so Elijah (1 Kings 17:21) and Elisha (2 Kings 4:34) are depicted as stretching themselves full length on the corpses of the boys they are depicted as bringing back to life.

When one reads that people bring little children to Jesus, not for healing, but simply for his touch (Mark 10:13, 16), one is perhaps reminded of how, in our celebrity culture, people seek tangible contact with a powerful or famous or revered "other." They line up, or jostle one another, in hopes of shaking the hand of the prime minister or president, or touching or being touched by the rock star or the pope. In the Greco-Roman world, implicit in the accounts of healing touch was the widespread idea that power resides in and emanates from certain individuals or certain objects powerful either in themselves (magnets, stones, plants) or when inscribed (amulets) or sculpted (statues). Thus, the woman with the hemorrhage is healed when a mere touch of Jesus' garment releases power that stops the flow (Mark 5:28–30). In a generalizing statement, the evangelist reports that the sick, having heard of Jesus' healings, throng to him, seeking to touch him (3:10) or even just "the fringe of his cloak" (6:56), as the woman did. The Lukan version of Mark 3:10 explains that power was going forth from Jesus and healing people (Luke 6:19).

These are persistent traditions. After a famous fourth-century Christian orator named Prohairesios delivered an impressive speech, the hearers kissed him on the hands and feet and licked his chest because they thought him possessed of divine potency (Eunapius, *Lives of the Sophists* 148). At about the same time, the bodily remains of Jesus' supreme early followers, the martyrs, begin to be regarded as possessed of healing power; such "relics" then come to figure prominently in medieval Christian piety.

Daemons/demons

The words of a potent person also have power, as was indicated earlier. It is words, not touch or objects or gestures, that are the power in the second basic kind of healings in the New Testament gospels: the casting out of demons or evil spirits. In Greek the word *daimon* has both good and bad connotations; however, especially through Jewish and Christian usage it acquired the strictly negative sense evident in the English "demon." The term "evil spirit" is familiar to Bible readers from the story of Saul and David (1 Sam. 16 and 18). The author of Mark uses these two terms with almost equal frequency and even interchangeably (e.g., 7:25–30).

Several passages in Mark (1:32, 34; 3:11) are general statements of demon expulsion, with no mention of symptoms. Other passages describe symptoms, sometimes briefly, at other times in detail, much more so than in the healing accounts considered thus far, and usually more graphically than in the parallel versions in Matthew and Luke. One symptom some of these sufferers display is preternatural knowledge. The man with "an unclean spirit" in Mark 1:24 knows Jesus is "the Holy One of God." Other "unclean spirits" identify him as "the Son of God" (3:11). They shout this out, as they fall down before him. The behavior of two other sufferers is more violent, of the kind we today associate with mental illness (5:2–10) or epilepsy (9:17–18, 20–22). In the first case the man goes naked, howls and bruises himself with stones, and frustrates efforts to subdue him. He too reveals Jesus' identity, shouting "at the top of his voice" that Jesus is the "Son of the Most High God." In the second case, the son of a distraught father has "an unclean spirit" that renders him mute, convulses him, and throws him to the ground, where he rolls about "foaming at the mouth," grinding his teeth, and becoming rigid.

The report that a Syro-Phoenician woman, after pleading with Jesus to heal her daughter, finds the girl lying in bed, the demon departed (7:30), also suggests agitated behavior as a sign of the unclean spirit's presence. Other, sometimes similar symptoms are reported in various ancient accounts, both pagan and Christian: falling down, with eyes rolling and mouth foaming (Lucian, *Lover of Lies* 16); falling on the ground, stripping off one's clothes (*Acts of Thomas* 64); speaking in an unnatural voice, staring with a strange gaze, or laughing or weeping inappropriately, or singing or talking to oneself (Philostratus, *Life of Apollonius* 3.38; 4.20).

Today we would likely ascribe such behavior to epilepsy, or think of those thus afflicted as mentally ill. In the nineteenth century various New Testament scholars attributed the same view to Jesus, saying that in treating these persons as demon-possessed Jesus was simply accommodating himself to the thought world of his time whereas he actually knew better. In assessing such a view one does well to keep in mind the warning contained in a book by the late Henry Cadbury entitled *The Peril of Modernizing Jesus* (1937). There is no evidence to support the ascription of modern conceptions of illness, mental or otherwise, to Jesus. Indeed, as another well-known New Testament scholar, David Friedrich Strauss, demonstrated in his *Life of Jesus* (1835–36), the New Testament gospels present Jesus as at one with his times in believing in demon possession. Since for him and for others in his world, conscious beings are involved, rather than impersonal forces, words are therefore appropriate in confronting them. Identities and names then become crucial.

Names

Though, in our world, one may not give much thought to names, one sees, on reflection, their importance, indeed their power. We recognize the importance of having "a good name." Advertisers know how crucial names are to product identity. A misdeed by a company official can give a firm "a bad name." We worry that the electronic dissemination of one's name (or government number) may lead to unwanted intrusion or leverage on our lives. In the ancient world names were at least as important, if not more so. Readers of the Bible may recall how a new name signifies a change in status. Abram becomes Abraham and Sarai becomes Sarah (Gen. 17:5, 15). Jacob is renamed Israel (Gen. 32:28); Peter becomes Simon's new name (Matt. 16:18). To authenticate Moses to the Israelites, God reveals the sacred name YHWH (Exod. 3:13–15), which they are later instructed not to profane (20:7), a commandment echoed in the prayer ascribed to Jesus: "hallowed be your name" (Matt. 6:9//Luke 6:2).

To learn another person's name is to enter into relation with him or her and to behave accordingly. So, too, with respect to deities or other powerful beings in the ancient world. Once the inhabitants of Lystra think they have identified Barnabas and Paul as Zeus and Hermes, they begin the procedures to offer sacrifice appropriate to those deities (Acts 14:11–13).

Knowing a name may also bestow power. The "magical" papyri are filled with names whose power the practitioners seek to invoke, among them various names of the Jewish deity and names of Jewish angels and Christian saints as well as the name of Jesus. Josephus (*Antiquities* 8.47) tells of a fellow Jew named Eleazar who knew a ritual to expel demons; along with other means, the ritual invoked the name of Solomon, the king noted in the Bible for wisdom, and then in subsequent Jewish tradition for occult lore. Eleazar would place to the nose of the sufferer a ring containing a root said to be specified by Solomon, and as the sufferer smelled the root, Eleazar would draw the demon out through the person's nostrils, whereupon Eleazar would utter Solomon's name and recite spells attributed to Solomon, adjuring the demon not to return – an unwelcome prospect described in one of the Jesus sayings (Matt. 12:43–45//Luke 11:24–26).

No such elaborate rituals or use of material means are recorded in New Testament reports or accounts of demon expulsions. In the case of Jesus' followers, it is the power of his name that compels the demons (see chapter 7 below). In the Gospel of Mark, names or identities figure in virtually all of the exorcism accounts. As was pointed out earlier, the demons know who Jesus is and identify him by name ("Jesus of Nazareth," 1:24), or status ("Holy One of God," 1:24; "Son of God," 3:11), or both ("Jesus, Son of the Most High God," 5:7). In identifying and naming Jesus, the demons might be seen as warding off his power, countering it with the power inherent in knowing his name – to no avail, however, for Jesus' power is greater, as the demons recognize and acknowledge. The question "What have you to do with us?" (1:23; 5:7) voices their resentment of Jesus' intrusion on their territory. "Have you come to destroy us?" (1:24) and "I adjure you by God, do not torment me" (5:7) give expression to an anxiety that proves well founded. By commanding them to be silent (1:25; 3:12), Jesus counters any power that knowledge of his identity might confer. Even at a distance (7:29), or without knowing their names (5:8; 9:25), he commands the spirits to depart from those they afflict (1:25, 27, 34).

Demonic power

In several of the healing accounts in Mark where demonic power is not expressly mentioned, certain words suggest its presence. In the healing of the deaf man who has difficulty speaking, we are told that (translating literally) "the bond of his tongue was loosed" (7:34) – as though some hostile power had been binding it. One is not surprised then that, in seeking to heal the man, Jesus looks up to heaven, that is, to God, for power to counter the evil force, and "sighs" or "groans" as he wrestles with it (7:34). In healing a leper, Jesus, we are told, is "moved with pity" (1:41). But some ancient manuscripts read "was angered" – as though by a malevolent power causing the disease. In the Lukan version of the healing of Peter's mother-in-law, Jesus "rebukes" the fever (4:39) – again as though it were a hostile power.

Some scholars have argued that the Greek verb (*epitimān*) translated by the NRSV, here and in Mark 1:25, as "rebuked" requires a more forceful rendering in view of usage in the Greek translation of the Hebrew Bible in contexts that refer to God's subjugating the primeval waters of chaos, or in certain Dead Sea scrolls referring to evil spirits. In the New Testament accounts Jesus would therefore be "subjugating" or "subduing" the fever or the unclean spirit. Jesus' power over the unclean spirit is also seen more clearly if one renders the Greek imperative *phimōthēti* (1:25) as "Silence!" (E. J. Goodspeed, *An American Translation*) or "Hold your tongue!" (E. V. Rieu, *The Four Gospels*), or more colloquially, "Shut up!" – all of which convey the sharp tone of the Greek. The same Greek verb is used later when Jesus silences the storm, as though it too were an evil power (4:39).

The evangelist's depiction of Jesus as a powerful exorcist would have struck a responsive chord among many in antiquity, where such persons were familiar figures. An exorcist described in Lucian of Samosata's mid-second-century satire of wonder-workers is an imposing figure who, after engaging in dialogue with spirits as Jesus does, threatens them if they do not depart when he adjures them to leave the persons they are possessing (*Lover of Lies* 16). Several decades later Philostratus portrays Apollonius of Tyana as insulting a spirit (*Life of Apollonius* 2.4), as threatening another in a letter addressed to it (3.38), and as addressing another as a master would a worthless slave (4.20). Several of the "magical" papyri (7.396; 9.4; 36.164) call for the practitioners to "muzzle" (i.e., silence) the powers they address, using the same Greek verb employed in Jesus' command to the unclean spirit.

Power/powerlessness

Were the early readers or hearers of the Gospel of Mark to think of Jesus as only an exorcist or a healer or a miracle worker, however, they would be taking him out of the context of the gospel, as our exposition has been doing as well. And that would be to misunderstand Jesus as healer in the Gospel of Mark.

One of the dominant scholarly interpretations of the Gospel of Mark in recent decades has been that the gospel was written precisely to counter such a "divine-man" image of Jesus held by certain early Christians and represented in the miracle stories in the first nine chapters of the gospel. The evangelist records these traditions, to be sure, but balances them with other early Christian traditions that – quite contrary to the common Greco-Roman image of the miracle-worker – tell the unlikely story of Jesus the miracle-worker ending his days hanging helpless on a cross.

Whatever the evangelist's intentions, what is plain is that he (or she?) wove together these two basic strands of tradition – Jesus as powerful and Jesus as powerless – into a writing that

opens with the words "the gospel" – that is, "the good news" –
"of Jesus Christ" (1:1). Imbued with two millennia of Christian
celebration of the Easter endings of the four New Testament
gospels, modern readers may find it difficult to appreciate how
difficult it likely would have been for early readers of the story
of Jesus – accustomed to stories of divine and semi-divine
figures who wouldn't be caught dead on a cross – to discern in
the story of Jesus "good news." All four gospels, but especially
the Gospel of Mark, indicate that also in his lifetime foe and
follower alike fail to discern the "good news." Put another
way, they fail to understand, and indeed they misunderstand,
Jesus, and give mistaken answers to his question, "Who do you
say that I am?" (8:29).

Some puzzling commands by Jesus in some of the healing
stories provide clues to whom – or rather what – the evangelist
considered Jesus to be and why the author saw that identity or
role as "good news." First, there are the commands to demons
to keep silent about his identity (Mark 1:25, 34; 3:12). These
commands, we have seen, can be read as countering any power
such knowledge might confer on the demons. What they say
about Jesus is not erroneous, however: their identifications of
Jesus as "the Holy One of God" (1:24), "the Son of God" (3:11),
accord with similar "approved" statements about Jesus (1:11;
9:7; 14:62). Despite the command that the demons not repeat
their statements, once uttered they provide the reader with
important information about Jesus. Then there are the commands to those he has healed, or who have witnessed a healing,
to tell no one of it (2:43–44; 5:43; 7:36). Not every healing
account ends thus, and one of them concludes with Jesus in fact
telling a man he has healed to go tell his friends (5:19), which
only makes one wonder all the more why in other instances
Jesus would not want his good and wondrous deeds to be
known. Related to these commands are those in which Jesus
tells his disciples not to reveal that he is the Messiah (8:30) or

to say anything about the wondrous scene they have witnessed on the mount when Jesus is transfigured before their eyes (9:9).

These various commands were labeled "the Messianic Secret" by the German scholar William Wrede in a book by that title published in 1901. Other pertinent passages he pointed out are those in which Jesus' disciples are depicted as confused or mistaken or fearful about his person, purpose, and teaching (Mark 4:13, 40–41; 6:49–52; 7:18; 8:15–21, 31–33; 9:5–6, 30–32; 10:24–26, 35–40; 14:36–41). Although Wrede's view of the issues is today largely superseded by other readings of these passages, one owes him a debt of gratitude for calling attention to them. While the details in these passages are difficult if not impossible to verify historically, they are nonetheless "true to life" in depicting the mixed reception that charismatic figures commonly arouse.

Jesus as possessed?

Stark opposition to Jesus appears in a key passage in the gospel (3:22–30) in which certain religious authorities charge that Jesus' casting out of demons occurs because he himself has a demon named Beezebul or Beelzebul (3:22), or "an unclean spirit" (3:30), and casts out demons "by the ruler of the demons" (3:22). This passage is tucked into another that reports opposition from Jesus' own family (3:21, 31–35): thinking him mad (3:21), they come to take him under their wing (3:21, 31).

In addition to the direct parallels to these passages in the other New Testament gospels (Matt. 9:32–34; 12:22–32, 46–50; Luke 11:14–23, 8:19–21), the charges of madness and demon possession occur in other passages as well, separately or together. Jesus is identified with Beezebul (Matt. 10:25). It is said he has a demon (John 7:20), or he is a Samaritan and has a demon (8:48), or is mad and has a demon (10:20).

Wild, abnormal behavior is explained by reference to demon

possession in Mark 5:1–20. Does unusual behavior underlie
the charge against Jesus? His behavior toward outcasts and
women and in flouting certain religious prescriptions, as
reported by the evangelists, is indeed unconventional and
arouses hostility (e.g., Mark 2:7; 3:1–6), and a common way of
expressing hostility was to "demonize" the offending person or
object, a practice not unknown in our day (America's enemies
may label it "the Great Satan," for example). Some scholars
have suggested that as practitioners of "magic" used spells and
rituals to summon spirits into their service, perhaps entering a
trance ("madness") as they did, so too did Jesus – or at least
knowledge of such practices may have led to the charge that he
"had" a demon and used it to cast out demons. (Note the
pairing in John 8:48 of "demon" and "Samaritan," Samaria
having some associations with "magic" [see Acts 8:9–11].)

For the author of Mark, all such conceptions are misconcep-
tions, as is clear from the Jesus sayings he records in reply.
How, asks Jesus, can a kingdom stand if its ruler contends
against those over whom he rules, in this case Satan against
his subjects, the demons (Mark 3:23–26)? Rather, like one who
binds a strong man in order to plunder his house (3:27), Jesus,
having overcome Satan in the wilderness (1:12–13), compels
Satan's forces to obey him, driving them out of the humans
they afflict. The "spirit" he "has" is not Beezebul, but God's
spirit, which enters "into" him (1:10) and empowers him to do
the healings and other mighty deeds that signal God's reign is
"at hand" (1:14), ascendent over Satan's. That is indeed "good
news" (1:14).

Sickness and sin

Opposition to Jesus, and misunderstanding of him, is evident
also in another account of a healing, this time of "a paralyzed
man" (Mark 2:1–12). The story raises a question that continues

to worry, and perplex, sick persons today: the relation between sickness and sin. That question is bluntly posed in the Gospel of John in the story of Jesus' healing of a blind man: "Rabbi, who sinned, this man or his parents, that he was born blind?" (John 9:2; see chapter 5 below). In the Markan account of the healing of the paralyzed man, a connection between his paralysis and sin is implicit: before healing the man Jesus forgives his sin. That connection is not always made in the Bible. Sometimes no cause of a sickness is named (see, for example, 1 Kings 5:1; Mark 1:30; 5:25). In pagan healing accounts and medical literature, sickness and sin or death are rarely connected, but there are a few examples. For instance, the inscriptions from the famous Asclepius temple at Epidaurus in Greece include two in which the god heals persons despite their disbelief in, or even ridicule of, his healing power (texts in E. J. and L. Edelstein, *Asclepius* [1945] 1:230). On the other hand, a slave who lies about money given to the god by another slave is afflicted with that slave's brand-marks (ibid. 1:231).

Such a connection between sin and sickness or death is more common in Jewish tradition. For his lying and greed, Elisha's servant is afflicted with the leprosy with which Naaman had suffered before Elisha healed him (2 Kings 5). Other passages also recount sickness inflicted or threatened by God for sinning (Num. 12; 16:41–50; Deut. 28:15, 22, 27–28, 35, 59–61; 2 Sam. 12:15). These traditions persist in the New Testament (1 Cor. 11:29–30; Acts 5:1–11; 12:21–23). At the same time, however, God is depicted as the great healer (Gen. 20:17; Exod. 15:26; 2 Kings 20:5; Ps. 6:2, 30:2, 103:3; Isa. 19:22, 30:26), and turning to physicians is therefore seen at times as signaling lack of trust in God (2 Chron. 16:12).

That both sickness and healing should be ascribed to God – "I wound and I heal" (Deut. 32:39) – raised questions about the divine nature. Later passages therefore introduce a/the "Satan" (literally, a/the "adversary") as the instigator of afflictions seemingly arbitrarily imposed by God (cf. 2 Sam. 24 with 1 Chron. 21:1), although sometimes Satan is seen as acting as God's agent (Job 1:6–12; 2:1–6; cf. 2 Cor. 12:7–8). Ascribing sickness to demons would also be a way of addressing these same questions.

These various strands of Jewish tradition are woven together in the account of the healing of the paralyzed man in Mark 2:1–12. Indeed, the repetitions at Mark 2:5, 10 ("he said to the paralytic") have led some to think two stories – one about forgiving of sin, another about healing – have been brought together to form the present account. As it stands, it presents Jesus as exercising these two functions commonly ascribed to God. Thus, the religious experts ("scribes") see Jesus' pronouncement of forgiveness as "blasphemy," that is, as defaming God by usurping a divine prerogative: "Who can forgive sins but God alone?" (cf. John 10:33). Jesus' reply, here as often in the gospels (Mark 3:4//Luke 6:9; Luke 14:3; Matt. 12:27// Luke 11:19; Matt. 17:25), is an either/or question: Is it easier to forgive sins or to heal? The logic of the question is that of "the greater-to-the lesser": healing is harder to claim because it must be publicly demonstrated; if performed, however, it will validate the proclamation of forgiveness, which is not empirically observable. And insofar as sickness is associated with sin, in accord with notions current at the time, healing of the paralyzed man will constitute remission of sin for him.

After the man picks up his mat and departs, the amazed spectators glorify God – but readers will notice that it is Jesus who, it is said, exercises God's "authority on earth" (Mark 2:10).

Restoration of Israel

The opposition that this claim arouses in this account continues the theme of opposition to Jesus voiced earlier by a demon (Mark 1:24–26). Subsequently (2:24), it is voiced again by religious leaders, leading to plans to do away with Jesus for healing on the sabbath (3:6) and later to the charge of blasphemy (14:64), a charge first raised here in the healing of the paralytic (2:7). For others in the gospel, however, the praise they give to the God of Israel is praise for a restoration of Israel in fulfilment of God's promise to bestow wholeness through forgiveness of sin, healing of physical malady, and restitution of prosperity – in short, the coming of the reign of God (1:15):

I am going to bring it [Jerusalem] recovery and healing; I will heal them and reveal to them abundance of prosperity and security. I will restore the fortunes of Judah and the fortunes of Israel. . . . I will cleanse them from all the guilt of their sins against me. (Jer. 33:6–7)

And no inhabitant will say, "I am sick"; the people who live there will be forgiven their iniquity. (Isa. 33:24)

The reaction of people to the healing of the deaf man – "he even makes the deaf to hear and the mute to speak" (Mark 7:37) – is explicit in its recollection of ancient promises to Israel: "Then the eyes of the blind shall be opened, and the ears of the deaf unstopped" (Isa. 35:5).

The reaction of the crowds to Jesus' healings, seeing in them a restoration of Israel, brings to mind studies by E. E. Evans-Pritchard, Mary Douglas, and other anthropologists showing the close relation between what happens to individual bodies and to social bodies. A persistent theme in the New Testament gospels is that Jesus associates with social outcasts and persons on the margins of society. This, too, the religious experts depicted in the Gospel of Mark find objectionable (2:16). In responding to their objections, Jesus uses the language of sickness and healing: "These who are well have no need of a physician, but those who are sick; I come not to call the righteous, but sinners" (2:17).

Jesus' presence among "sinners" is an affirmation of God's acceptance of them, of their inclusion in Israel; it is a beginning

of a healing of the rifts and tears in the social body, another
manifestation of the dawning of the reign of God. So, also,
when Jesus touches the untouchable – a leper – and sends him
off to a priest for the required certification that his body is
indeed healed and he thus may be readmitted to the social
body (1:40–44; see Lev. 14:1–32); or when Jesus is defiled
(according to Jewish tradition) by physical contact with a
hemorrhaging woman (5:28; see Lev. 15:19–30) or defiles
himself by taking a dead person by the hand (5:41; see Num.
19:11–13, 31:19). In reaching out, touching, and healing these
individuals' bodies, Jesus reintegrates them into the social
body. He transgresses another boundary when he heals on the
sabbath (1:21–31; 3:1–5), again arousing opposition (3:2, 6).

Crossing of boundaries

In these various actions Jesus is crossing boundaries within
Judaism. In some of the healing stories he crosses the boundary
between Jew and non-Jew as well. In the Gentile (non-Jewish)
area of the Decapolis (literally, "Ten [Greek] Cities"), on the
eastern side of the River Jordan, Jesus restores to full participation in society a man deaf and impaired in his ability to
communicate with others (7:31–37). A decidedly Gentile area
of the Decapolis (the raising of pigs, ritually unclean animals
for Jews, is mentioned) is the setting for an even more dramatic
restoration of a social outcast to normal society (5:1–20). The
behavior of a man possessed by an unclean spirit is considered
so bizarre and threatening that people have attempted more
than once to fetter him, but to no avail: he wrenches the
chains apart and breaks the shackles. "No one had the strength
to subdue him." So he has been abandoned to a solitary
existence "among the tombs and on the mountains," where
day and night he howls and bruises his naked body with
stones. Upon hearing him identify himself to Jesus as "Legion"

(a Roman military unit of around 6,000 soldiers), "for we are many," readers today might be inclined to think of multiple personality disorder. For the people in the story, however, it is the demons who have possessed him that are the cause. After the demons have left the man (at the expense of a herd of pigs!), the townspeople hearing the news, come and find him seated, "clothed and in his right mind." Jesus then sends him home to his friends – to normal society. While Jesus' transgressions of boundaries provoke hostility among some of his fellow Jews, here the reaction of these non-Jews is fear, and a request to Jesus to depart.

Another boundary-crossing narrative is set to the west in the area of Tyre (and Sidon?) on the Mediterranean coast (7:24–30). The daughter of "a Greek [woman], a Syrophoenician by birth," has an unclean spirit (7:24–30). Jesus' gruff rejection of the desperate mother's initial request to heal her daughter is shocking to modern ears: "dogs" (non-Jews), says Jesus, are not to receive what is reserved for the children (Jews). This story comes, however, after a series of Jesus sayings that reject certain Jewish distinctions between "clean" and "unclean" that mark observant Jews off from Gentiles (7:1–23), and it precedes the healing of a non-Jew (7:31–37). While Jesus in rebuffing the mother does not reject the doctrine of Jews as God's chosen people ("the children"), the fact that he ultimately yields to what one might call her "doggedness" in pressing her suit is presented by the evangelist as another instance of boundary-crossing by Jesus.

Jesus says that it is her reply to his rebuff that changes his mind (7:29). In the parallel account in Matthew Jesus calls her stance "faith" (15:28; Greek, *pistis*). Other healing accounts in Mark also speak of the "faith" of those Jesus heals (5:34; 10:52), or of the faith of those who bring the afflicted person to him (2:5, "their faith"), or of the importance of "believing" (5:36; 9:23, 24; Greek, *pisteuein*). Since the Protestant Reformations, "faith" and "believing" likely suggest to persons in those traditions faith in Jesus Christ as savior from sin. In the healing accounts in Mark, however, "faith" is, rather, trust or confidence that Jesus can heal. This becomes clearer when one examines further the "messianic secret" mentioned earlier and the understandings, or rather misunderstandings, of who Jesus is, as these are set forth by the evangelist.

Who – what – is Jesus?

By chapter nine of the Gospel of Mark the reader knows that Jesus is a powerful healer, that demons know his true identity, and that his opponents are mistaken in thinking he is in league with demons when in fact it is God's own spirit that is "in" him. Still, one is puzzled that Jesus issues commands not to reveal his identity. These puzzlements become even more entangled as the story progresses, but then begin to unravel as the "secret" of Jesus' identity unfolds – but in a way that still mystifies his followers in the story.

As was mentioned earlier, Jesus is set apart from other healers of the time in ending up hanging, helpless, on a cross. The picture of Jesus as powerful healer in the first part of the gospel is haunted by his opponents' taunts at the crucifixion: "He saved others; he cannot save himself. Let the Messiah, the King of Israel, come down from the cross now, so that we may see and believe" (15:31–32). Jesus' crucifixion confirms their prior disbelief in any divine source of his power to heal. Jesus' followers too are stunned by what happens to him. The disclosing chain of events begins to unfold in a crucial scene set in the vicinity of Caesarea Philippi at the north end of the Jordan Valley (8:27–30).

Jesus asks his disciples, "Who do people say that I am?" The answers they give presuppose that Jesus is something more and other than the young man rejected in his hometown and unable to work any wonders there except healing a few people by laying on of hands (6:1–6). Elsewhere, however, the crowds that throng to him – the "people" envisaged in Jesus' question – regard him as one of God's prophets.

The "people" speculate that he is Elijah, risen from the dead to fulfill his role as the promised forerunner of the Day of the Lord (see Mal. 4:5–6; *Sirach* 48:10; Matt. 11:14; 17:10–13). Or he is John the Baptist, risen from the dead, as King Herod and others surmised (Mark 6:14, 16). This surmise, and the claim that John's powers were now operative in Jesus (6:14), would not occasion surprise in a world where the spirits of those who suffered an untimely death, as happened to John (6:17–29), were thought to linger on and be available to persons with the skill to summon them.

Since none of these answers is adequate, Jesus addresses the question of his identity to the disciples themselves, and Peter responds, "You are the Messiah" – a designation the evangelist leaves, significantly, undefined. What follows in the gospel, however, makes sense of Jesus' stern command not to say anything to anyone about him (8:30), that is, about his messiahship, because to do so before it is plain what *kind* of messiah he is can only result in misunderstanding.

That occurs in the sequel to Peter's confession. Jesus' predictions of his suffering and death, repeated three times (8:31; 9:31; 10:32–34), are too mind-numbing for his disciples to contemplate or comprehend, too dissonant with their sometimes confused but nonetheless unmistakable experience of his power. At Jesus' first announcement that he "must" suffer and die (a divine "must"), Peter's response is to take Jesus aside and "rebuke" him for such talk, whereupon Jesus calls Peter "Satan," possessed of a mind focused "not on divine things but on human things" (8:31–33). The second prediction produces incomprehension, but the disciples fear to ask for an explanation (9:32). Following the third prediction James and

John approach Jesus with a request for choice seats when Jesus will rule in glory, to which Jesus repeats, in another form, that he will suffer and die and that he came, not to be served, but to serve and give his life for others (10:35–45). Hardly the kind of messiah or king the two eager disciples fancy or expect.

One can hardly blame them. Have they not witnessed his healings and other displays of power? Have not Peter, James, and John just recently seen with their own eyes a glorious transfiguration of Jesus in the presence of Moses ("the law") and Elijah ("the prophets") (9:1–8)? Is it not the common expectation, expressed ironically in the taunt at the cross, that Israel's messiah and king will rule in power? Little wonder the disciples are bewildered.

They are not present, having fled when Jesus is arrested, but the reader is, when Jesus for the first time publicly acknowledges that he is the Messiah (14:61–62) – an acknowledgment that comes only after it has become clear that this messiah must suffer and die. The reader then also begins to understand why it is that Jesus has commanded his followers not to reveal he is the Messiah until after his suffering, death, and resurrection (8:29–33; 9:9, 31–32; 10:31–32).

The miracles at Jesus' baptism that designate Jesus as God's chosen one (1:11) are followed by the healings and other displays of power that signal that God's reign is drawing near. But it is the baptism of his death (10:38) – where Jesus is powerless – that the author of Mark depicts as the decisive victory over the sickness and demons and death that stand in contradiction of God's reign.

A wounded healer

To borrow a term coined by Henri Nouwen to designate the modern Christian minister, Jesus in the Gospel of Mark is a "wounded healer," one who, to paraphrase the author of

Hebrews (2:14–18), experienced, along with those he healed, the pain and suffering of human life and ultimately death itself, in one of its worst forms. The two streams of early Christian tradition brought together by the evangelist – Jesus as powerful and powerless – are represented by the fearful disciples, bewildered by their experience of both. The gospel ends on such a note (16:1–8). The women who come to Jesus' tomb on the third day after his death find his body gone and "a young man" present there who instructs them to tell Jesus' other followers that "He has been raised." Instead, the women flee "in terror and amazement" and tell no one, "for they were afraid" (16:8).

That the gospel should end thus is clear in the best manuscripts, and modern translations therefore conclude the gospel at chapter 16:8. However, they also print "shorter" and "longer" endings found in other manuscripts that provide more "satisfying" conclusions.

The longer one, familiar to readers of the King James Bible (16:9–20), depicts Jesus promising his followers invulnerability to snakes and poisons and the power to cast out demons and heal the sick. Various small religious groups, especially in the American south, take these promises literally, with members occasionally dying as a result. The Gospel of Mark's portrait of Jesus as healer – powerful yet powerless, healing yet himself wounded – is a sobering reminder of human vulnerability to the thousand natural shocks that flesh is still heir to, and the ambiguous ending of the gospel accords with the ambiguities attending sickness and healing to the present day.

Chapter 3

Jesus as Healer: The Gospel of Matthew

Readers who come to Matthew from Mark will recognize much of the terrain but will also find much new territory to explore. Most of what is found in the Gospel of Mark will be found in Matthew as well, including most of the healing stories. Missing are only the casting out of an unclean spirit (Mark 1:23–28), the healing of the deaf man (7:32–37), and the restoration of the sight of the blind man of Bethsaida (8:22–26). However, as if by way of compensation, the author has included other, similar healing accounts or summaries.

Jesus restores the sight of two blind men (Matt. 9:27–31) and casts a demon out of a mute (9:32–33), which leads into a charge that Jesus casts out demons by the ruler of the demons (9:34). In the actual Matthean parallel to the Markan version of the Beezebul controversy, two very similar healings lead into the controversy, but they now happen to one man, who is both blind and mute (12:22–24), rather than to three with these afflictions as in Matthew, chapter nine. The Markan account (10:46–52) of a blind man named Bartimaeus whom Jesus heals as he leaves Jericho appears in Matthew as the healing of two blind men, both unnamed (20:29–34). (The two very similar healings of two blind men [9:27–31; 20:29–34], the first a retelling of the second based on Mark, are what scholars call a doublet. Both versions will be considered later.) The summary account of healings in Matthew 15:29–31 appears where the story of the healing of the deaf man does in Mark (7:31–37) and offers a heightened parallel to it. Moreover, the author of Matthew rearranges certain of the healing accounts found in

Mark, grouping them with other miracle stories in chapters eight and nine. Both the author of Matthew and the author of Luke also drew on source material that scholars call "Q" (from the German word *Quelle*, "source"), which includes healing accounts (Matt. 8:5–13//Luke 7:1–10; Matt. 12:22//Luke 11:14) and material pertaining to healing (Matt. 11:2–6//Luke 7:18–23; Matt. 12:43–45//Luke 11:24–26).

To take a rough modern analogy, one might compare the author of Matthew to a figure most moviegoers scarcely notice as the credits roll by. This is the editor, the person who, as much as the director or producer, creates the illusion of "story" from the various filmed sequences delivered to her or him. The evangelist, like the scribe of Matthew 13:52, puts together "new" (Jesus traditions) and "old" (prior Jewish traditions) to produce in the decade 80–90 CE another version of "the good news." He writes out of the midst of and for an audience different from that of the author of Mark – perhaps a Christian community in Antioch consisting of persons of both Jewish and Gentile origin (cf. Gal. 2:11–14; Acts 11:19–26). The basic Markan picture of Jesus as powerful-then-powerless healer persists, but various features are modified and others added to produce a distinctly Matthean portrait.

Teaching and authority

One of these distinctive features is that Jesus teaches much more than he does in Mark. It is not that the author of Mark does not conceive of Jesus as teacher. He refers to Jesus as teacher twelve times and to what he teaches five times; he portrays him teaching fifteen times, and presents blocks of that teaching in chapters four and thirteen. But the narrative overshadows the teaching, whereas in Matthew the two balance each other off, with large blocks of narrative regularly

followed by large blocks of teaching. Jesus' role as healer is
thus less prominent than in Mark.

Jesus' authority as teacher is also differently authenticated
in Mark and Matthew. In Mark Jesus teaches in the synagogue
in Capernaum, and people "were astounded at his teaching, for
he taught them as one having authority, and not as the
scribes" (1:21). What this might mean becomes clear in what
follows (1:22–28), one of the few Markan passages that did not
make it into Matthew. Jesus casts out a demon, whereupon the
spectators are amazed and keep asking one another, "What is
this – a new teaching with authority! He commands even the
unclean spirits and they obey him." Thus it is Jesus' healing
power that bestows authority on his teaching.

In Matthew, on the other hand, it seems to be the very
teaching itself and the form in which it is couched that move
the people to draw the contrast between Jesus' teaching and
that of the scribes (7:28–29). This pronouncement comes not
in the Capernaum synagogue, as in Mark, but as the conclusion to the Sermon on the Mount (chapters 5–7), in which
Jesus contrasts his teaching with what "was said to those of
ancient times" (5:21; similarly, 5:27, 31, 33, 38, 43), that is, the
handing on of traditions in the manner of the scribes. To these
traditions Jesus opposes his "But I say to you" (5:22, 28, 32, 34,
38, 44), introducing a series of radical contrasts between them
and his own teaching. These antitheses are followed in the
Sermon by two more chapters of challenging sayings. It is,
then, in the next two chapters, eight and nine – collections of
miracle stories – that Jesus' authority over hostile powers of
nature, sickness, and demons is demonstrated. Thus, as one
scholar, Julius Schniewind, has observed, Jesus is presented as
messiah in word (chapters 5–7) and in deed (8–9), with the
virtually identical introduction (4:23) and conclusion (9:35)
that frames these chapters referring to both teaching and
healing.

The combination of these two, teaching and healing, sets Jesus apart from other healers of the time, for whom only healing is generally reported. The evangelist also seems to want to distance Jesus from run-of-the-mill healers who employ gestures as well as metals, stones, herbs, parts of animals, and other materials considered potent against disease. Thus he excludes from his gospel the Markan story of the healing of the deaf man (Mark 7:31–37) and the healing of the blind man of Bethsaida (8:22–26), both of which include such details. And the Matthean version of the Markan summary of casting out of demons (Mark 1:32–33) adds that Jesus did the casting out (solely) "with a word" (8:16). Jesus' mastery in debate would presumably set him apart also from the Jewish exorcists mentioned in Matthew (12:27) and Luke (11:19) ("Q" material) who possess no such talent.

Fulfiller of prophecy

The evangelist also sets Jesus apart by citing what he sees as ancient prophetic (i.e., divinely inspired) testimony to Jesus, something other healers lack and that the other New Testament evangelists often merely imply is true of Jesus. The author of Matthew, like a scholar searching the scriptures (cf. 13:52), finds in them predictions proving that Jesus, in his birth, teaching, miracles, suffering, and death, is God's chosen one. Thus after presenting a series of healings (8:1–16), the evangelist comments, "This was to fulfill what had been spoken through the prophet Isaiah, 'He took our infirmities and bore our diseases'" (8:17, citing Isa. 53:4). The "messianic secret" is given similar treatment. After Jesus performs many healings, and orders those healed "not to make him known" (12:16), the evangelist explains that this is in fulfillment of the prophet Isaiah's description of God's servant, who "will not wrangle or cry aloud, nor will anyone hear his voice in the streets" (12:19, citing Isa. 42:2) – that is, he will carry out God's work away from the public gaze. A jarring statement, this, in view of the crowds that throng to Jesus; but it provides scriptural (i.e., divine) warrant for the commands to silence for which the author of Mark offers no such explicit explanation.

Rather jarring, too, is that the Isaiah passage also states that the servant will proclaim "justice to the Gentiles" and that the Gentiles will hope in his name (Matt. 12:18, 21, citing Isa. 42:1 and 42:4 [in a Greek version of this latter verse]). Jarring because it is only in Matthew that Jesus, on sending out his disciples to preach, exorcise, and heal, commands them to restrict themselves to "the lost sheep of the house of Israel," avoiding Gentiles and Samaritans (10:5–6). And it is only in Matthew that Jesus tells the Syro-Phoenician woman, "I was sent only to the lost sheep of the house of Israel" (15:24). Not until the very end of the gospel does Jesus, now risen, command his disciples to go and make disciples of all *ethné*, the Greek word commonly translated "Gentiles" (28:19; NRSV: "nations"). Nonetheless, as in Mark, reaching out to Gentiles has begun already in Jesus' healings, as precedent, as it were, for his post-resurrection command and in anticipation of it. The evangelist retains Markan accounts of healings of Gentiles: the demoniac living among the tombs (Matt. 8:28–34), though the evangelist changes the location, presumably so the pigs will have to run only the six miles from Gadara to the Sea of Galilee rather than the thirty-three miles from Gerasa as in Mark; and the daughter of the Syro-Phoenician woman (15:21–28). The evangelist also includes from the source material ("Q") he shares with the author of Luke the story of the healing of the son or servant (Matt.) or slave (Luke) of a Roman soldier ("a centurion") (Matt. 8:5–13// Luke 7:1–10).

Restoration of Israel

As in Mark, Jesus is also presented as restoring Israel to wholeness. After Jesus heals "the lame, the maimed, the blind, the mute, and many others," the crowds "praised the God of Israel" (15:30–31). When John the Baptist, now in prison, dispatches his disciples to inquire whether Jesus is "the one who is to come" – that is, God's messiah – Jesus' reply is that "the blind receive their sight, the lame walk, the lepers are cleansed, the deaf hear, the dead are raised, and the poor have the good news brought to them" (11:2–5) – in fulfillment of ancient hopes (see Isa. 29:18–19).

Not everyone sees it that way. As in Mark, Jesus' healings arouse opposition, seen in a plot against him (Matt. 12:14) and in the accusation that Jesus casts out demons through the ruler of demons (12:22–24). Ultimately, Jesus predicts the transferring of God's reign from Israel to a people that produces the fruits demonstrating that God rules over them (21:43). At the crucifixion in this gospel the breach is complete (in a passage, 27:25, that has played a significant role in Christian anti-Jewishness over the centuries). Thus it is that Jesus establishes a new community, the *ekklēsia*, or "church," a term that occurs only in Matthew (16:18; 18:17) among the New Testament gospels. It is this *ekklēsia* that, after his death and resurrection, he commissions to go and make disciples of the Gentiles, baptizing them, and "teaching them to obey everything that I have commanded you" (28:19–20). What such obedience might mean may be found in the gospel itself, including the healing stories.

Jesus as healer: Matthean characteristics (Matt. 8–9)

One marked characteristic of the healing stories in Matthew is their terseness. Most of the graphic details that impart such

color to the Lukan and (especially) Markan versions have
been pruned away by the author of Matthew. The reader's
attention is thus focused more sharply on certain Matthean
themes: Jesus as Messiah and Lord of the church in fulfillment of prophecy; faith and "little faith"; and discipleship.
Put another way, the healing stories serve another Matthean
theme – Jesus as teacher – for in their Matthean versions they
instruct the reader or would-be disciple regarding faith, discipleship, and who Jesus is. In the healing of the leper (8:1–4)
that opens the two chapters of miracles, descriptive details
have been trimmed (contrast Mark 1:40–45). What remains,
and stands out, is the request for healing and the healing
command, and the implicit suggestion that the person the
leper addresses as Lord can heal also in the present day.
Similarly, in the later account of the stilling of the storm it
becomes clear that this same Lord can deliver those who
follow him into "the boat," that is, who cast their lot with
him in the church as disciples (8:23–27), whatever the cost
(8:18–22).

In the next healing account in chapter eight (8:5–13) Jesus is
also addressed as Lord, this time by a Roman centurion
seeking healing of his son or servant; the omission of details
(cf. Luke 7:1–10) again focuses attention on the dialogue and,
this time, on faith. The source material ("Q") employed by the
authors of Matthew and Luke represents Jesus as stating that
in Israel he has not found such faith as this Gentile possesses;
but the conclusion in Matthew adds further emphasis: "Go; let
it be done for you according to your faith." Faith also comes to
the fore later in the Matthean version of the healing of the
Syro-Phoenician woman's daughter (Matt. 15:21–28); here the
evangelist, instead of his usual shortening, for once expands on
the Markan source (Mark 7:24–30): the addition (Matt.
15:23–24) heightens the distance between Jesus the Jew and
the woman, a non-Jew. All the more remarkable then is her

persistence, which leads Jesus to exclaim, "Woman, great is your faith! Let it be done for you as you wish."

The next healing in chapter eight (8:14–15), that of Peter's mother-in-law, is decidedly terse. Though it might be assumed that in Peter and Andrew's house both of them (as well as others) would be present (as the Markan source states), in Matthew only Jesus and the sick woman are mentioned, thus focusing attention on the two of them, and leading into a summary statement about Jesus healing many demoniacs and sick persons and quoting the fulfillment passage from Isaiah noted earlier (8:16–17).

After the ensuing instruction about discipleship and the stilling of the storm (8:18–27) mentioned earlier come two more healing stories, both sharply abbreviated versions of the Markan originals. In the first, the Gadarene demoniac (8:28–34), the one demoniac has become two, a Matthean kind of doubling observed already in other accounts. Thus, even though the Markan dialogue in which the demoniac identifies himself as "Legion" (Mark 5:8–9) is omitted, the demons can speak in the plural ("us"). But that a whole herd of swine should be impelled into the sea by only two demons becomes less credible. Moreover, the omission of the Markan details about the poor sufferer's exclusion from society means that his healing is not seen as a restoration to society. Instead, when the townspeople come out to see what has happened they see, not "the demoniac sitting there, clothed and in his right mind" (Mark 5:15), but "him" (Matt. 8:34), that is, Jesus.

If the focus is on Jesus in this account, in the next, the healing of the paralytic (9:1–8), it shifts subtly to Jesus' followers. The omission of the Markan report (Mark 2:4) that the man's friends dig through the roof in order to lower him down in front of Jesus means that Jesus' comment that "Jesus saw their faith" (Matt. 9:2) is what literary critics call unmoti-

vated. That for the evangelist, faith is not the key element in
the story becomes evident in the conclusion when the crowds
glorify God, "Who had given such authority" to forgive sins –
not "on earth," that is, to Jesus, as in Mark (2:10), but "to
human beings" (Matt. 9:8). When the reader comes to the two
scenes where Jesus grants his church the power to "bind" and
"loose" on earth (16:13–19; 18:15–26), then the phrase "to
human beings" acquires a specific referent, namely, the followers of Jesus. In their "binding" and "loosing" they could
point to this story as the basis of their actions, even as, in their
not fasting, they could point to Jesus' subsequent defense of his
followers over against the disciples of John the Baptist
(9:14–17). Intervening, however, are two stories about Jesus
associating with "sinners" (9:9–13), examples of his healing of
rifts in society observed already in Mark.

The two chapters of miracle stories conclude with four
healing accounts. The fourth of these, the healing of a mute
demoniac (9:32–34), is found only in Matthew, as was noted
earlier. The other three are, again, abridged versions of the
Markan accounts. Shorn drastically of its Markan details
(5:21–43), the Matthean version of the healing of the hemorrhaging woman (9:20–22) leaves Jesus and the woman alone in
private conversation, with the result that Jesus' encouraging
words, "Take heart, daughter; your faith has made you well,"
focus attention on her faith.

Though the sharply abridged version of the raising of Jairus'
daughter (9:18–19, 23–25) makes no explicit mention of faith,
the greatness of Jairus' trust in Jesus' power is evident from a
Matthean alteration in the Markan text: the daughter is not
merely "at the point of death" (Mark 5:23), she has in fact just
died. Nonetheless, the father appeals to Jesus for help; and, as
in Mark, Jesus proves worthy of his trust and brings the girl
back to life. The Markan conclusion in which Jesus orders the
witnesses to say nothing about the miracle (Mark 5:43) is

omitted here, and the news of what has happened spreads (Matt. 9:26).

The same occurs as a result of the third healing, restoration of the sight of two blind men (9:27–29), found only in Matthew, as was mentioned earlier: despite Jesus' command to tell no one, they leave and report what has happened. The agreements and similarities between this healing and the one in Matthew 20:29–34 suggest that the earlier one is a retelling of the later one, which, in turn, is an abridgment of the Markan version (Mark 10:46–52). In chapter twenty, interestingly, the evangelist omits (Matt. 20:34) the words of the Markan Jesus: "Go; your faith has made you well" (Mark 10:53). Here in chapter nine, however, near the end of a collection of healing stories in which the faith of the sick person has been seen to be prominent, Jesus says to the two blind men, "According to your faith let it be done to you" (Matt. 9:29).

The fourth and final healing account (9:32–34) leads, as was noted earlier, to opposition by the religious leaders, sparked by the crowd's amazed assertion, "Never has anything like this been seen in Israel" (9:33). The crowds throng around Jesus as he goes about teaching, "proclaiming the good news of the kingdom and curing every disease and every sickness" (9:35).

Disciples as healers

It is Jesus' compassion for these crowds, "like sheep without a shepherd" (9:36), that introduces another essential aspect of Jesus as healer: empowering his disciples to heal. This happens in the next chapter. The Matthean version of this empowerment shows some significant differences from Mark. Not only does Jesus give his twelve key followers "authority over unclean spirits" (Mark 6:7//Matt. 10:1), in Matthew he also commands them to proclaim the very message he proclaims –

"the good news, 'The kingdom of heaven has come near'"
(10:7; cf. 4:17) – and to perform the same sorts of healings that
have just been reported of him: "Cure the sick, raise the dead,
cleanse the lepers, cast out demons" (10:8).

Four of the evangelist's favorite themes – discipleship, faith
and "little faith," and Jesus as teacher – occur in a later healing
account, when we observe the disciples seeking to carry out
Jesus' command to heal – but in vain (17:14–21). The Markan
account is again stripped to essentials: a dialogue between
Jesus and the father of the epileptic boy, the casting out of the
demon, and Jesus' instruction of his disciples. Rather than
attributing the disciples' inability to heal to their failure to use
prayer, as in Mark (9:29) – what might be termed a mistake in
technique – here in Matthew Jesus switches roles from healer
to teacher and explains (17:20) that the disciples failed because
of their "little faith" (*oligopistia*), a distinctive Matthean term
with which Jesus has reproached his disciples several times
earlier (6:30; 8:26; 14:31; 16:8). Had they but "faith the size of a
mustard seed," they could perform wonders – indeed, "nothing
will be impossible" for them (17:20). What is impossible for the
disciple is possible with God, however, (cf. 19:25–26).

Jesus' disciples have over the centuries practiced healing,
whether of sickness (see chapter 7 below) or of those suffering
social ills – hunger, thirst, lack of clothing, displacement,
imprisonment (Matt. 25:35–40) – those whom Jesus terms "the
least" of his brothers and sisters (25:40). The Matthean Jesus
has been for them model, teacher, Lord. At times, however,
some of his followers have sought to force Jesus' ancestral
brothers and sisters – Jews – to become brothers and sisters in
faith, that is, Christians, and have appealed, not without some
warrant, to various passages in the Gospel of Matthew itself for
support of their actions. Having themselves experienced Jesus
as powerful healer and bringer of wholeness, they seem not to
have perceived that in Matthew, as in the other New

Testament gospels, Jesus is also the wounded healer, who seeks not to lord it over others, imposing his will on them, but, rather, to serve them, even to giving his life for them (20:24–28). These same followers perhaps fail to note that, according to the New Testament gospels, it is Romans, not Jews, who put Jesus to death, on a charge of subversion ("King of the Jews," Mark 15:26//Matt. 27:37, Luke 23:38, John 19:19). Perhaps ignoring those passages in Matthew (and elsewhere in the New Testament) that leave to God final, eschatological judgments about who "belongs" and who doesn't (Matt. 7:21–23; 13:24–30; 25:31–46), they have thus worked hurt rather than healing, as if (to borrow a Matthean phrase) in fulfillment of Jesus' warning to be on guard lest an evil spirit, once expelled, return, bringing also "seven other spirits more evil than himself" (12:43–45).

Chapter 4

Jesus as Healer: The Gospel of Luke

"Luke, the beloved physician." Thanks to these few words in the Letter to the Colossians (4.14) an early Christian named Luke became in ancient times the patron saint of physicians and surgeons. In our time a society formed some decades ago to foster healing ministry, originally in the Anglican/Episcopal church, took the name the Order of St. Luke, and at various times writers of fiction have taken pen in hand to provide "the beloved physician" fuller treatment than the New Testament writers did. Around these same few words as well as other New Testament references to "Luke" (Philemon 24; 2 Tim. 4:11) clusters a considerable body of scholarly literature debating whether "Luke" was the author of a full quarter of the New Testament – the Gospel of Luke and the Acts of the Apostles – and, if so, whether he was indeed a physician.

No author is named in the Acts. The "we" passages (Acts 16:10–17; 20:5–8, 13–15; 21:1–18; 27:11–28:16) are no exception; they tell us little except that the author, following literary convention, wants readers to know he had experienced the kind of sea travel described in those passages. Nor is any author named in the Gospel of Luke, a trait it shares with the other three New Testament gospels. The superscriptions of all four – "The Gospel According to ... " – are all later additions. Ultimately, the authors of all four remain anonymous, like so many of the early Christians (cf. 2 Cor. 8:18–19). Reading between the lines of the gospels, however, one can learn a fair bit about the evangelists, virtually none of it undisputed, however.

Medical terminology

From the medical terminology in the Gospel of Luke, W. K. Hobart (*The Medical Language of St. Luke* [1892]) concluded that the author must have been a physician – a view supported by the distinguished historian of ancient Christianity, Adolf von Harnack (*Lukas der Arzt*, English translation, *Luke the Physician* [1907]), as well as other scholars. In 1920, however, Henry J. Cadbury of Harvard Divinity School showed that the supposedly technical medical language of the author was the common property of many authors who were definitely not physicians, even as today, thanks to increasingly sophisticated journalism and the health newsletters published by various medical schools, medical terms such as ebola, AIDS, HDL and LDL, amniocentesis, or *in vitro* come up regularly in ordinary discourse.

What the evangelist's use of some of the medical terminology of his day tells us is that he had a good vocabulary of the kind one would expect of someone with a good Greek education. One observes this as well in the way he revises some of the more homely Greek in the Gospel of Mark but also in the many instances where he quietly "fixes up" problems in Markan narratives, including the healing stories. One might compare him to a present-day manuscript or copy editor, unsung experts in language who work behind the scenes improving authors' manuscripts. For example, the conclusion of the Markan version of the healing of a leper might, on quick reading, leave one wondering whether it was the healed leper or Jesus who goes out and begins to "spread the word" (of the healing? the gospel?) (1:45). The Lukan version (5:15) removes at least some of the Markan unclarity by stating simply that "the word about him spread abroad" and many gathered to hear Jesus and be healed. This wording also clears the leper of any charge of having disobeyed Jesus.

Similarly, in contrast to Mark 1:24–26, the demon in the
Lukan account (4:33–34) obeys Jesus' command to be silent.
Sick persons also obey Jesus' commands, details lacking in
Mark: the healed paralytic does indeed go home as bidden by
Jesus (Luke 5:24–25//Mark 2:12); the man with the withered
hand does stand up, as Jesus has directed (Luke 6:8//Mark 3:3).
The author of Mark does not tell us how the blind man at
Jericho, on hearing Jesus coming, finds his way to Jesus on his
own – note how those standing by offer no help and indeed
discourage him (Mark 10:46–50). The Lukan version explains
what happened: Jesus orders the blind man to be *brought* to
him (18:40).

Use of sources

The author of Luke is much more than a manuscript editor,
however, fixing up another's lapses and smoothing away rough
edges. Like the writer of Matthew, he is a creative author in
his own right. Above all, he is a remarkable storyteller whose
renderings of the Good Samaritan (10:30–35), the Prodigal Son
(15:11–32), and other tales from everyday life are familiar even
to many with little or no acquaintance with the Bible. Among
the four New Testament evangelists, he and the author of John
(see chapter 5 below) are the only ones that make explicit
mention of the sources each employed. The author of Luke
introduces his version of the "good news" with a carefully
weighed and precisely worded statement of how he proceeded
in his research and writing. This prologue (1:1–4) provides
crucial insight into how the healing stories and other materials
he took from his sources fit into the overall structure of the
Gospel of Luke and its sequel by the same author, the Acts of
the Apostles (see Acts 1:1).

First, the evangelist takes note of the "many" who have
already sought to write "an orderly account" of certain events

(1:1): he is not the first to try a hand at what he is setting out to do. Second, he wants the reader to see that these events are to be viewed as fulfillments (1:1), that is, of scripture and of the divine will, a theme prominent in Matthew, as we have seen, and one that this evangelist will likewise pursue in various ways. Third, the traditions about these events go back to the very first eyewitnesses and servants of the word (1:2); that is, even though the author himself was not "there," he wants readers to believe that he has garnered the traditions from those who were are trustworthy. Fourth, the evangelist, having done his own careful research on the whole sequence of events, is here presenting his own (better) account of them (1:3). Finally, he is doing this for the benefit of someone named Theophilus who, though he has already received some instruction about these events, will now receive assurance that what he has been taught is trustworthy (1:4). Whether the "Theophilus" to whom both the gospel and the Acts of the Apostles (1:1) are addressed is an actual person or an ideal reader (the name means, literally, "God-lover") has been a subject of scholarly debate but is, ultimately, immaterial: whoever is in need of "assurance" or "certainty" (Greek, *asphaleia*, translated by the NRSV as "truth") about the events alluded to by the evangelist is addressed by his prologue and what follows it.

Luke–Acts as history

What follows is a two-volume history of these events, that is, the whole Christian movement beginning with its humble origins, indeed reaching all the way back to the first human (3:38), and concluding with its steady, divinely inexorable spread from Jerusalem through various Mediterranean lands to the very capital of the Empire, Rome itself (Acts 28:14–31; cf. Acts 1:8). Scholars have long observed that the author of Luke, alone among the evangelists, writes in the tradition of Greek and Roman historians. This is evident beginning already in the tightly structured prologues to the Gospel and the Acts, which recall the prologue by Herodotus (fifth century BCE), "the father of history," to his lengthy account of the war Persia waged against Athens and Sparta in the fifth century BCE.

This is the result of the research of Herodotus of Halicarnassus, presented so that the things that took place may not become lost from human memory with the passage of time and so that great and wondrous deeds praised both by Greeks and barbarians may not lose their lustre, and, moreover, the reason why these went to war with one another. (*History* 1.1)

The author of Luke stands in this same tradition of historiography when he provides introductions to the well-known "Christmas story" – the account of Jesus' birth (2:1–4) – and the ministry of John the Baptist (3:1–2) that situate these very precisely in place and time within the Roman Empire. The stage is now no longer the villages and towns of an obscure Roman province, as in Mark and Matthew, but "all the world" (2:1; Greek, *oikoumenē*), and the time, as Victorian stage directions used to say, is "the present" – some time in the eighties of the first century CE when Greeks, Romans, and other peoples of the far-flung Empire might wonder where to place on the religious spectrum these people coming to be "called Christians by the general public" (Tacitus, *Annals* 15.44; cf. Acts 11:26). It is not surprising that the Roman historian Tacitus, writing at the beginning of the second century CE, would view with suspicion what he regarded as "a pernicious superstition" that revered a man – "Christus" – who suffered the most shameful death Romans could inflict (*Annals* 15.44). Luke–Acts seeks to set the record straight, offering "assurance" (*asphaleia*) that there is nothing to fear and much to gain from the Christians and their Christus. That same Christus was crucified, yes – but he is also powerful to heal in his compassion, especially for the outcasts of society, not only in the past (the Gospel of Luke) but also in the present, through his followers (the Acts of the Apostles).

Lukan healing accounts

In the book of Acts, one of those followers, Peter, delivers a long sermon to other Jews in Jerusalem on a day that later Christians came to call Whitsunday or the Festival of Pentecost in celebration of the giving of the Holy Spirit on the fiftieth (Greek: *pentēkostē*) day after Easter. The sermon aptly summarizes the evangelist's treatment of the miracle stories he found in his sources: Jesus was "a man attested to you by God with deeds of power, wonders, and signs that God did through him among you" (Acts 2:22). Later, when addressing Gentiles in Caesarea on the Mediterranean coast, Peter summarizes the message about Jesus similarly, but now specifies those wondrous deeds as healings: "how God anointed Jesus of Nazareth with the Holy Spirit and with power; how he went about doing good and healing all who were oppressed by the devil, for God was with him" (10:38).

In contrast to the author of Matthew, the author of Luke uses fewer of the Markan healing accounts, as a result of his passing over a large chunk of Mark (6:48–8:26; what scholars call the "Great Omission") that contains four healing stories or summaries: healings at Gennesaret (Mark 6:53–56); the daughter of the Syro-Phoenician woman (7:24–30); the deaf man (7:31–37); and the blind man of Bethsaida (8:22–26). Like Matthew he includes (from "Q") the healing of the centurion's slave (Luke 7:1–10//Matt. 8:5–12), the healing of a deaf mute (Luke 11:14//Matt. 12:22 [deaf and blind]), and material pertaining to healing (Luke 7:18–23//Matt. 11:2–6; Luke 11:24–26//Matt. 12:43–45).

Luke, like Matthew, also contains healing materials not found either in Mark or Q, what scholars call "L" material:

Jesus "cured many people of diseases, plagues, and evil spirits, and had given sight to many who were blind" (7:21); he heals a widow's son (7:11–17), a disabled woman who for eighteen years had been unable to stand erect (13:10–17), a man with "dropsy" (i.e., edema, an accumulation of fluid in some part of the body [14:1–6]), ten lepers at once (17:11–19); and he restores the ear of the high priest's slave cut off by one of Jesus' followers when Jesus is taken into custody (22:50–51). In addition, only in the Gospel of Luke (8:2–3) do we hear that some of Jesus' women followers "had been cured of evil spirits and infirmities." Among those named is Mary Magdalene, "from whom seven demons had gone out," a tradition that resurfaces in the later Longer Ending of Mark (16:9).

Healings as "assurance"

These various accounts are put in the service of the "assurance" the evangelist has promised Theophilus in the prologue: more than in the other gospels, the healings and other miracles provide evidence that God, or God's spirit, is at work in Jesus. This evidential function of Jesus' healings is seen in the prominent place the evangelist gives to the acclamations that conclude the healings:

Amazement seized all of them, and they glorified God and were filled with awe, saying, "We have seen strange things today." (5:26)
Fear seized all of them; and they glorified God, saying, "A great prophet has risen among us!" and "God has looked favorably on his people!" (7:16)
And all were astonished at the greatness of God. (9:43a)
When he laid his hands on her, immediately she stood up straight and began praising God. (13:13)
Immediately he regained his sight and followed him, glorifying God; and all the people, when they saw it, praised God. (18:43)

Each of the healings thus makes clear that Jesus heals "by

the finger of God" (as Jesus states in the Lukan version of the Beezebul controversy), from which one is to conclude that "the kingdom of God has come to you" (11:20). The "finger" imagery recalls the contests in miracle-working between Israel's champions, Moses and Aaron, and Pharaoh's magicians. When the magicians are unable to duplicate Aaron's plague of gnats, they conclude, "This is the finger of God!" (Exod. 8:19). Seeing (as the adage has it) is believing. A Jewish contemporary of Jesus, Philo of Alexandria, regarded sight as superior to the other senses, less deceptive than they (*On Abraham* 57, 60, 150, 153, 156, 158–62, 166); in one passage he specifically contrasts "seeing" and "hearing" (*On Flight and Finding* 208). The author of Luke seems to hold a similar view. "Blessed are the eyes that see what you see!" says Jesus in Luke (10:23), in contrast to the Matthean Jesus who continues, "and your ears, for they hear" (13:16). Before Jesus replies to John the Baptist's query whether he is "the one who is to come," he heals many people of various afflictions (7:21), and then instructs John's disciples to report what they had "*seen* [i.e., healings] and heard" (7:22), a sequence that appears in reversed order in Matthew ("what you hear and see" [11:4]).

Nonetheless, hearing is also important for the evangelist. Like the other three New Testament evangelists, he presents Jesus not only as a healer and miracle-worker but also as a teacher, thus setting him apart from other healers of his day. At times the link between his healing and his teaching is more pronounced than in Mark or Matthew. For example, the Markan account of the healing of a leper concludes with a summary statement (lacking in Matthew) of Jesus' popularity (1:45). The author of Luke, however, explains that crowds came "to *hear* him and to be *cured* of their diseases" (5:16). Whereas in Mark (3:8–11) people come to Jesus only for healing, in Luke they come "to *hear* him and to be healed of their diseases" (6:17). Later on, Jesus in Luke both teaches *and* heals (9:11), whereas in the parallel passages he either teaches (Mark 6:34) or heals (Matt. 14:14).

Fulfiller of prophecy

Through passages such as these the evangelist evidently wants readers to see that Jesus has become what he said he would be – a teacher and a healer – thus fulfilling the ancient Hebrew scripture that he reads in the synagogue in his home village of Nazareth and then applies to himself. Jesus will "bring good news to the poor," "proclaim release to the captives and recovery of sight to the blind," and freedom to "the oppressed" (Luke 4:18–19, quoting Isa. 61:1 as it appears in ancient Greek translations of the Hebrew Bible).

Readers at this point in the story know that the Holy Spirit has descended on Jesus at his baptism (Luke 4:27) and that "filled with the power of the Spirit," he has "returned to Galilee" (4:14) and to his home village of Nazareth (4:16), where he pronounces that the ancient prophecy has been fulfilled in himself (4:21). Readers are therefore not surprised when he also applies to himself the prophet's statement, "The Spirit of the Lord is upon me" (4:18, citing Isa. 61:1). The townspeople are surprised, however; indeed, they are "amazed at the gracious words that came from his mouth," and they speak "well of him" (6:22). On second thought, however, seemingly reflecting on the contrast between what they regarded as his grandiose claims for himself and his well-known, everyday origins, they ask one another, "Is not this Joseph's son?" (4:22).

The theme of opposition to Jesus, familiar from the other gospels, is thus introduced, here in his home village. Jesus summarizes it succinctly, in a passage found only in Luke, that refers tacitly to his healings (4:23): "Doubtless you will quote to me this proverb, 'Doctor, cure yourself!'" Then, in a subtle reference to village pride or village rivalries, he continues: "And you will say, 'Do here also in your hometown the things that we have heard you did at Capernaum.'" "Capernaum? What things?," the reader may well ask, for Capernaum has received no mention to this point; the evangelist, usually so careful, has nodded and forgotten (or ignored) that he has not included the Markan passage (1:21–28) that reports "the things" – various healings – done in Capernaum. The narrative assumes that the villagers know, however, and also that they will recognize the proverb about the physician (some form of it is attested in various ancient sources, both pagan and Jewish).

Jesus, Elijah, and Elisha

This rejection of Jesus as teacher and healer in the place where he grew up – "no prophet is accepted in the prophet's hometown" (Luke 4:24//Mark 6:4, Matt. 12:57) – leads into a discourse (Luke 4:24–27) that presages his rejection in his home country as well. It echoes a familiar theme in the Hebrew prophets, that Israel rejects the prophets the Lord sends to it (e.g., Isa. 6:6–10; Jer. 7:23–26, 25:3–7; 2 Chron. 36:15–16; cf. Luke 11:49–51; Matt. 23:34–35; Luke 13:34// Matt. 23:37; Acts 7:51–53). The examples Jesus cites here (found only in Luke) are the famous prophet Elijah and his almost equally famous disciple, Elisha (4:25–27). Of their various deeds the ones Jesus singles out are those that have to do with Gentiles. In relating Elijah and Elisha traditions to Jesus, and specifically to Jesus as healer, the evangelist implies or recalls or imitates various aspects of what the scriptures tell about these two famous prophets. Thus, implicitly or explicitly he casts Jesus in their mold, indeed, as their (superior) fulfillments; at the same time he sets Jesus apart from other miracle-workers credited with raising the dead.

One example of the latter from a pagan source may serve as illustrative of others. Apuleius of Madaura (born *c.* 123 CE) tells the story of an Egyptian prophet (Latin *propheta*) who places an herb on the mouth of a dead man, another on his chest, then, turning east, prays to the rising sun, whereupon the dead man's chest begins to show movement, his blood begins to flow, and, now breathing fully, he gets up and begins to speak (*Metamorphoses* 2:28–29). With stories such as this in mind Gentile readers of Luke would hear with interest what Jesus says to the Nazareth synagogue about Elijah and Elisha, for both stories concern Gentiles like themselves.

During a long famine in Israel, says Jesus, Elijah is sent (i.e., by God), not to anyone in Israel, but to a Gentile widow in a town (Zarephath) in the Gentile region of Sidon near the Mediterranean coast (Luke 4:22). Omitted from the Lukan account is what happens next (see 1 Kings 17:8–24). In the account in 1 Kings, the widow meets Elijah at the gate of the town. Later, her only son falls ill and dies. She reports this to Elijah, accusingly, as if the presence of this "man of God" has brought about her son's death because of her sin (17:18). Thereupon, Elijah restores her son to life and (concludes the account) "gave him to his mother" (17:23). Similarly, when, further on in Luke, Jesus enters the town of Nain, there meets him at the gate a widow who, along with a crowd of mourners, is accompanying the body of her only son to its resting place (7:12). Jesus halts the procession, restores the son to life, and "gave him to his mother" (7:15), the very words (in Greek) that appear in the Greek translation of the Elijah story (17:23). There is no mention of the woman's faith, even as in the Elijah story the woman exhibits anything but trust that Elijah can help her in her plight.

Along with these similarities between the Jesus and the Elijah stories, there are significant differences. In contrast to the life-restoring gestures employed by Elijah (1 Kings 17:21;

see chapter 2 above) – and the procedures employed by Apuleius' Egyptian prophet – Jesus brings the son back to life simply by ordering him to rise (Luke 7:14). Moreover, the Lukan account, unlike the Elijah story, concludes with acclamations by the awed spectators: "A great prophet has arisen among us!" and "God has looked favorably on his people!" (7:16).

Jesus, Moses, Elijah, and Elisha

These are weighty pronouncements. Various Jewish sources attest to a belief current in Jesus' day that, while prophecy might have ceased, a prophet would someday appear to set things right in Israel. In addition to biblical passages to this effect (Ps. 74:9; cf. 1 Macc. 4:46, 9:27, 14:41), the *Community Rule*, one of the most important of the Dead Sea Scrolls, attests an expectation of "the prophet" along with "the messiahs [or: anointed ones] of Aaron and Israel" (*Community Rule* [1QS] 9:6). One of the bases for such a hope was God's promise in Deuteronomy 18:15–18 to raise up for Israel a prophet like Moses, a passage cited by the author of Luke–Acts (Acts 3:22; 7:37) and reflected in the words spoken by the voice from heaven in the transfiguration scene, "Listen to him!" (Luke 9:35; cf. Deut. 18:15). These words, and the presence of Moses in this scene, imply that Jesus is in fact the prophet like Moses who, among the various miracles credited to him, showed himself to be a healer (Num. 12:10–15; 21:8–9). This is one of those fulfillments of scripture that the evangelist promised would provide Theophilus assurance concerning the instruction he had received (Luke 1:1, 4).

The prophet Elijah is also present in the transfiguration scene (Luke 9:30). He represents another current of hope for a final, ultimate prophet, one the author of Luke also finds fulfilled in Jesus. Unlike Moses (Deut. 34:5–6), Elijah does not die but is taken up bodily into heaven (2 Kings 2:11), giving rise to the hope that he would someday return. This hope found expression in a prophetic utterance preserved in the Book of Malachi: "Lo, I will send you the prophet Elijah before the great and terrible day of the Lord" (Mal. 4:5; cf. 3:1). According to the New Testament evangelists, people speculate that Jesus is in fact Elijah (Luke 9:8//Mark 6:15; Luke 9:19//Mark 8:28, Matt. 16:14). We have seen, in the raising of the widow's son, that the author of Luke models Jesus as healer on Elijah as healer. He does the same with Elijah's disciple, the prophet Elisha. In an account that parallels Elijah's restoring a son to life, Elisha also brings a son back to life (2 Kings 4:18–37). There is, however, no explicit reference to this feat in Luke. Rather, in the discourse in the synagogue in Nazareth, Jesus refers to Elisha's healing, at a distance, of a Gentile military commander's leprosy (Luke 4:27; see 2 Kings 5:1–14). Further on in the gospel we see that Jesus too heals – at a distance – the slave of a Gentile military commander (Luke 7:1–10). Later, as if to outdo Elisha in healing (even as he surpassed Elijah), Jesus heals not one, but ten lepers (17:11–18).

There are also other ways in which the evangelist seems to imply that Jesus is superior to these two famous prophets. When a certain Samaritan village rejects Jesus, his disciples James and John ask if they should "bid fire come down from heaven and consume them" (9:52–54) – that is, as Elijah, not once, but twice, had called down fire to consume those who opposed him (2 Kings 1:9–12), or as Elisha's curses of small boys who jeered him resulted in two bears' mauling forty-two of them (2 Kings 2:23–24). Jesus denies his disciples' request: he is not that kind of prophet.

A similar distancing comes to light also in his relation to the man cast in the role of Jesus' forerunner, John the Baptist. John, for his part, seems to cast Jesus in the role of fiery prophet when he proclaims that his own baptism is with water but the one who comes after him (i.e., Jesus) will baptize with fire (Luke 3:17). When, instead, John in Luke (7:18) hears from his disciples of Jesus' healings (two are reported just prior, in 7:1–15), and that people are therefore proclaiming Jesus as "a great prophet" (7:16), he in his puzzlement sends his disciples to ask Jesus, "Are you the one who is to come?" (7:19) – that is, you're not behaving as I expected God's promised one would behave. Jesus' reply in Luke follows a statement that "Jesus had just then cured many people of diseases, plagues, and evil spirits, and had given sight to many people who were blind" (7:21), thus anticipating and substantiating his reply. The reply turns out to be a recital of Jesus' healings and of his proclaiming of "good news" to the poor (7:22). Jesus as the promised prophet brings healing, not the fire of judgment.

Corporate healing, and role reversals

As in the other gospels, so also in Luke Jesus' healing is of the social body as well as of individual bodies. In Luke, however, such social healing figures much more prominently. It appears already at the beginning of the gospel in Mary's song (the "Magnificat") announcing a coming reversal of roles for the strong and the weak, the rich and the poor, those who eat their fill and those who go hungry (1:46–55). In the synagogue in Nazareth Jesus announces, as we have seen, how he will reach out to the poor and oppressed (4:18). The number of Beatitudes in Luke, in the Sermon on the Plain (6:20–23), is half that in the Sermon on the Mount (Matt. 5:3–12). Moreover, the Matthean versions of two of the Beatitudes are less "physical" than the Lukan forms: "Blessed are the poor *in spirit*" (Matt. 5:3) versus "Blessed are you who are poor" (Luke 6:21). "Blessed are those who hunger and thirst *for righteousness*" (Matt. 5:6) versus "Blessed are you who are hungry now" (Luke 6:21).

As a result, the Lukan Beatitudes focus attention on the literally poor and hungry, on those who weep and are hated "on account of the Son of Man [i.e., Jesus]." The blessings on these socially marginalized and outcast persons is then contrasted in Luke, but not in Matthew, with the rich, those who "are full now," and those of whom "all speak well" (Luke 6:20–26) – on these, woes are pronounced.

As in the other New Testament gospels the healing stories in Luke show the sick restored in health and thus to society. It was indicated earlier that the evangelist includes a number of the healing stories found in Mark and Q. He also includes various of their accounts of Jesus' mingling with social outcasts. However, it is in what scholars have come to call the Lukan Travel Narrative (9:51–18:14) – Jesus' journey to Jerusalem – that we encounter stories found only in Luke (what scholars call "L" material) that, one after another, feature role reversals or Jesus reaching out to embrace persons on the fringes of society or excluded from it.

The rich man who plans to build bigger barns to hold his bumper crop but then dies the very night he congratulates himself on the good life that awaits him (12:13–21; "L") is immediately contrasted with those who do not worry about material goods (12:22–31, "Q"). Zaccheus, the rich tax collector, receives Jesus into his home and promises to give half of his goods to the poor and to compensate fourfold anyone he may have defrauded – whereupon Jesus restores this "sinner," "one of the lost," to the Jewish fold by pronouncing him a "Son of Abraham" (19:1–10; "L"). By contrast, the rich young ruler, a respected member of society, cannot bring himself to give up his riches to the poor (18:18–30//Mark 10:17–31, Matt. 19:16–30). Another such person, a rich man who enjoys gourmet meals every day while a poor, sick beggar languishes at his gate, finds their roles eternally reversed when he dies (16:19–31; "L"). A Pharisee, the very model of piety and proud of it, is compared unfavorably with a tax collector so burdened with guilt he can barely breathe a prayer for God's mercy (18:9–14; "L"). To those who accuse Jesus of associating with "tax collectors and sinners" (15:1–2; cf. Mark 2:15–16//Matt. 9:10–11, Luke 5:29–30), Jesus tells parables of "the lost" whom God seeks to reclaim: the lost sheep (Luke 15:3–7; "L"), the lost coin (15:8–10; "L"), the lost son (15:11–32; "L"). Those who give banquets should "invite the poor, the crippled, the lame, and the blind" (14:12–14; "L"), and those who seek choice seats at banquets will find themselves relegated to a lower place, while those who choose the lowest places will be invited to move up (14:7–10; "L").

These role reversals prefigure still another reversal, the most significant of all, not only in Luke but, as we have seen, in all the New Testament gospels: Jesus the powerful healer of ills – individual and social – ends up powerless, in the grip of his opponents. As in Mark and Matthew, Jesus has predicted this turn of events three times (Luke 9:22//Mark 8:31, Matt. 16:21; Luke 9:44//Mark 9:31, Matt. 17:22; Luke 18:31–33//Mark 10:32–34, Matt. 20:17–19). Both in Matthew and Luke ("Q" material) he also predicts the divisive effect his healings and teaching will have (Luke 12:51, "division"//Matt. 10:34, "sword"). In addition, the Lukan Jesus speaks of this discord as "fire" he casts on the earth (12:49; "L") and then in the same breath of the baptism he must undergo (12:50; "L"; cf. Mark 10:38), that is, the death he must suffer.

These are ironic fulfillments of John's prediction that Jesus would baptize "with the Holy Spirit and with fire" and burn up the chaff he has winnowed from the grain (Luke 3:16–17// Mark 1:8–9, Matt. 3:11–12). Jesus himself undergoes the baptism John predicted of others, and not till that is accomplished will the baptism of Spirit and fire occur (see Acts 2:3–4); and not till the final judging will fire sift the evil from the good (Luke 16:23–26; "L").

Demonic powers

These are events of cosmic significance, and it is perhaps not surprising, then, that the author of Luke accords a cosmic power – the devil or Satan – a larger role in illness and in the Jesus story generally than the gospels studied thus far. The evangelist includes various of their accounts of expulsions of demons. While he omits passages that seem to portray Jesus struggling with illness as with a hostile force (Mark 1:41, 7:34; see chapter 2 above), it is only in Luke that Jesus heals Peter's mother-in-law by "rebuking" (or "subjugating") her fever (4:39). Moreover in a story found only in Luke, the cause of an illness that has kept a woman bent double for eighteen years is said to be "a spirit" (13:11), and, in responding to the charge that he healed her on the sabbath (13:14), Jesus speaks of her as having been "bound for eighteen long years" by Satan (13:16).

In summarizing Jesus' work as a healer, the author of Luke–Acts describes those he heals as "oppressed by the devil" (Acts 10:38). Accordingly, when the 70 disciples return from their mission of healing and announcing the imminent advent of God's reign (Luke 10:9), they report that in Jesus' name "even the demons submit to us" (10:17; "L"). Jesus responds (in words reflected in magnificent passages in Milton's *Paradise Lost*, 1.44–49, 740–46) that while they were casting out demons he was watching "Satan fall from heaven like a flash of lightning" (10:18; "L"; cf. Isa. 14:12). Satan, having seen Jesus withstand the three tests he has put to him (4:9–12), departs "from him until an opportune time" (4:13; "L"). That time comes when he enters Judas (22:3; "L"), who then goes off to arrange to betray Jesus (22:4). When that happens, Jesus' most outspoken follower, Peter, will be "sifted" by Satan (22:31; "L").

However, as Milton's Satan acknowledges, God is more powerful than he, and (in Peter's words at Pentecost) "God raised him [Jesus] up" (Acts 2:24), another evidentiary miracle, demonstrating, this time, that Jesus' death was "according to the definite plan and foreknowledge of God" (2:23), revealed in the scriptures (Luke 24:26–27; "L") but not perceived there by Jesus' followers till after his resurrection (24:13–35; "L") This is another fulfillment, providing to Theophilus further assurance of the validity of the instruction he has received (1:1, 4): God keeps the promises made to Israel through the scriptures. If many in Israel reject the fulfillment of the promises, these are then held out to Gentiles. There have been hints of that in the gospel, as in the other gospels. However, it is in the sequel to the Gospel of Luke, the Acts of the Apostles, that Theophilus will see that story unfold and his instruction further substantiated as Jesus' followers proclaim the message about Jesus, first to Jews and then to Gentiles, as well as heal in his name (chapter 7 below).

Chapter 5

Jesus as Healer: The Gospel of John

In comparing the various ways in which the New Testament gospels portray Jesus as healer, scarcely any reference has been made so far to the Gospel of John. There are good reasons for this. While the figure of Jesus as healer in the first three gospels is distinct in each, it is clear that the authors nonetheless drew on common sources. Even when they turn to other Jesus traditions, as do the authors of Matthew and Luke, these traditions are generally similar to one another. The result is three writings that are closely related, often very closely, in language and structure, as becomes evident when they are laid out side by side in what is called a "synopsis" (literally a "together view," for which reason scholars refer to them as "the Synoptic gospels" or, simply, "the Synoptics").

Turning to the Gospel of John, one sees that, at its most basic, the portrait of Jesus as healer is, to be sure, the same as in the Synoptic gospels: Jesus the powerful one meets death as Jesus the powerless crucified one. Beyond that, however, even a cursory reading of John reveals how significantly it differs from the Synoptics. The sentences flow easily, and the language is uncomplicated (students learning New Testament Greek commonly begin their reading of the New Testament with John, once they have acquired the rudiments of the language). The apparent simplicity dissipates, however, the more one delves into the gospel. As someone aptly put it, the Gospel of John is shallow enough to wade through and deep enough to drown in.

Some problems in interpretation are quite obvious. For

example, the author places Jesus' cleansing of the Jerusalem temple at the beginning of Jesus' ministry (John 2:13–22) rather than at the end, where the Synoptics have it. Whereas the other three evangelists show Jesus moving in his ministry from Galilee to Jerusalem within the space of a year, the author of John has him moving back and forth between Galilee and Judea over the course of three years. In Mark (15:25) Jesus is crucified on the Passover, in John, however, on the day of preparation for the Passover (19:14). Hence, at his last meal with his disciples, Jesus washes their feet and makes no mention of bread and "body," as he does at the Synoptists' passover meal; in John such "eucharistic" language appears instead after the feeding of the multitude in chapter six (6:53–58).

In that chapter the reader may observe how puzzled are the actors in the Johannine drama by what Jesus says to them and the claims he makes for himself. While readers may also find much that puzzles and perplexes, and much to ponder, they are in important ways better off than the various personae in the gospel itself. This is because the evangelist imparts to readers crucial knowledge about Jesus that many of the characters in the gospel are not privy to. That makes readers "insiders" while most of the persons in the gospel itself are "outsiders."

Perhaps the most critical insider information concerns Jesus' origins. Is he (as the Synoptics have it) from Nazareth (thus John 1:45; 18:5)? Or is he, rather, from Judea (4:43–45; 7:1)? Outsiders are certain he is from Galilee, therefore he cannot be the Messiah, for do not the scriptures state that the Messiah will come from Bethlehem in Judea (7:52, 42)? (Compare Matt. 2:1–12, Luke 2:4–7.) On the other hand, say the outsiders, whereas they "know where this man is from," "when the Messiah comes, no one will know where he is from" (7:27; similarly, 9:29). Readers know, however, as part of their insider

information: he is "from above," "not of this world" (8:23),
ultimately, neither from Galilee nor Judea nor Bethlehem. The
outsiders, not perceiving this, and therefore not in fact
knowing where Jesus is from, unwittingly and ironically testify
that he is the Messiah, whose origins, they say, no one will
know.

It is clear, therefore, that the question of Jesus' identity –
rooted in his origins – is central in this gospel, more prominently and more openly than in the Synoptics where it is
implicit much of the time but is posed explicitly only by Jesus
to his closest followers ("Who do people say that I am?") and
by Jewish and Roman officials when he is in custody (Mark
14:61//Matt. 26:63, Luke 22:67; Mark 15:2//Matt. 27:11, Luke
23:3). In John the question of Jesus' identity is crucial also in
the healing stories, where the insider–outsider scenario figures
prominently. In contrast to the numerous miracle stories in
the Synoptic gospels, only seven longer accounts and two
shorter ones appear in John, all in the first eleven chapters. Of
the seven, four are healing accounts. In addition, we are told
that Jesus is able to discern people's thoughts (2:25) and their
life histories (4:16–19, 29), an element that appears in one of
the healing accounts (5:6). A number of passages (2:23; 3:2;
6:26; 7:31; 11:47; 12:37; 20:30) also inform readers that Jesus
performed many miracles including healings (6:2; 9:16).

Signs/*Sēmeia*

Once again, however, John is different, beginning already with
the two Greek words the evangelist uses for "miracle." The
first of these is "work" (Greek, *ergon*; e.g., 7:21; 10:32) or
"works" (*erga*, e.g., 7:3; 9:3–4; 10:25, 32, 37–38; 14:10–12;
15:24), which the author also uses to denote Jesus' teaching
(14:10) or even the entire mission entrusted to him by the
Father (17:4). The second term the evangelist uses, namely,

"sign" (sēmeion; 2:18; 4:54; 6:14, 30; 10:41; 12:18) or "signs" (sēmeia; 2:11, 23; 3:2; 6:2, 26; 7:31; 9:16; 11:47; 12:37; 20:30), he restricts to miracles, however.

There are certain clues in the gospel that suggest the author may have drawn on a collection of miracle stories, a sēmeia or "signs" source. Thus, Jesus' turning of water into wine in Cana of Galilee is said to be "the first of his signs" (2:11), and his healing of the royal official's son, also in Cana of Galilee, is designated as "the second sign that Jesus did after coming from Judea to Galilee" (4:54). The numbering of the signs in this way, the similarity in the structure of both accounts, the same geographical setting of both, the fact that the second sign (the healing story) begins by referring explicitly to the first sign (water into wine) and to its geographical location (4:46), and then concludes by referring to the location again – all of these suggest that the healing account may have followed the water-into-wine miracle in a "signs" source. Another pointer to a signs source is the conclusion of chapter twenty, where the author states that "Jesus did many other signs ... which are not written in this book" (20:30) – a surprising statement at this point in the gospel since so much else intervenes between it and the last of the signs, the raising of Lazarus from the dead (11:1–41), or any mention of signs whatever (11:47; 12:37). Such a statement, would, however, be an appropriate conclusion to a collection of signs employed by the author in reporting healings and other miracles.

A number of scholars have contended that the author's designation of Jesus' wondrous deeds as "signs," sēmeia, sets them apart from pagan "miracles." The author's treatment of the sēmeia is indeed distinctive, in comparison not only with pagan sources but also with the other three New Testament gospels, as we shall see. But the term itself is not what accounts for the distinctiveness. The term is part of the vocabulary shared by pagans, Jews, and Christians of the

time. The basic meaning of *sēmeion* is "that which identifies," a "sign" that points beyond itself. The pagan writer
Plutarch (*Life of Pericles* 6:2–4) gives as examples of *sēmeia*
in everyday life the ringing of a gong, the light of a beacon
fire, and the shadow of the pointer on a sundial. Their sight
and sound are not significant – signifying – in themselves.
Rather, says Plutarch, their signifying nature is a matter of
social convention: people have agreed that they will function
to signify. A schoolbell, a fire siren, a traffic light are, one
might say, modern *sēmeia* – signs summoning, alerting,
directing. (Traffic lights, one may recall, are also called traffic
*sig*nals.)

In the world of the evangelist an extraordinary happening
such as a healing could also function as a *semeion*. But
agreement on what was signified did not come so easily as
with a gong or a beacon. This is evident in Plutarch's discussion of extraordinary *semeia*, and it becomes quite apparent in
the Gospel of John – not surprisingly, for different individuals,
and especially different (and differing) social groups, may well
be quite at variance in the way they view the same extraordinary event. In the first place, was the event really extraordinary – or could it perhaps be explained as in fact not out of
the ordinary, if properly understood? On this point, we learn
that Jesus' *sēmeia* produce the amazed reaction (John 6:14;
7:21; 9:32) that we have observed as a stock element in healing
accounts, and the *sēmeia* are assessed as extraordinary also by
outsiders (3:2) and opponents (11:47) in the gospel.

But of what, then, are the *sēmeia* a "sign"? What do they
signify? For the evangelist this is the crucial question, as is
evident from the fact that his accounts of the *sēmeia* commonly lead into extended debates about their significance,
debates that are not found in the other New Testament
gospels. For the evangelist, and for the insiders both in the
gospel and those who stand outside it as readers, the *sēmeia*

tell who Jesus is, his true identity as opposed to the false conceptions held by the outsiders.

These identifications come in two forms – shorthand and longhand, one might say. The short versions occur, typically, in the "I am" sayings characteristic of this gospel. "I am the light of the world" (6:12; 9:5; similarly, 12:46). "I am ... the life" (11:25; 14:6). "I am the bread of life" (6:35, 41, 48); "I am the bread that came down from heaven" (6:41; similarly, 6:50); "I am the living bread that came down from heaven" (6:51). The Johannine healing accounts, together with the ensuing dialogues, are the "longhand" versions of the "I am" sayings, depicting in dramatic fashion how these *sēmeia* are indeed "signs" signifying that Jesus is truly light, life, and sustenance, the very essence of health and healing.

Healing: believing and seeing

The first healing in the Fourth Gospel is, as we have seen, the "second sign" in Cana of Galilee (4:46–54). A royal official from Capernaum appears there begging Jesus to come and restore his dying son to health. When Jesus puts him off with a brusque reply, the official simply repeats his plea, whereupon Jesus tells him to return home, because "your son will live." On the way home, the official is met by his slaves, who inform him that his son lives and, as it turns out, had begun his recovery at the very hour Jesus had said he would live. The similarities between this story and the "Q" account of the centurion's son or servant (Matt. 8:5–13//Luke 7:1–10) examined in the two preceding chapters suggest that all three are variants of a single incident. (The Syro-Phoenician woman's insistent pleading for her daughter in the face of Jesus' rebuff [Mark 7:24–30//Matt. 15:21–28] also comes to mind.)

The Johannine version is a *sēmeion* pointing to Jesus as the one who gives life, a theme announced already in the third chapter of the gospel and culminating in the raising of Lazarus from the dead in chapter eleven. Jesus' rejection here of believing based on seeing the wondrous (4:48) anticipates the healing of the blind man in chapter nine and the question of who really "sees." Here, the official, on the one hand, believes – without seeing – when Jesus tells him his son will live (4:50). On the other hand, once this trust in Jesus' ability to heal is confirmed by the report that his son does indeed live, we are told that "he himself believed, along with his household" (4:53). Similar statements occur in Acts, reporting conversions to Christianity (Acts 18:8; cf. 10:2; 11:14; 16:15, 31, 34), and scholars have suggested that this statement in John, though placed in the time of Jesus, represents rather the time of the composition of the gospel (c. 90–100 CE) and conversion to Christianity, that is, believing in Jesus as the Messiah. Such faith, only implicit here at most, is made explicit in subsequent healing accounts in John.

Do you want to be made well?

It is in the next *sēmeion* (5:1–18) that a theme familiar from the Synoptics – opposition to Jesus as healer – first appears. The provocation is also familiar: healing on the sabbath. In typical Johannine fashion, the question of Jesus' identity again emerges as well as, implicitly, the identity of the person healed. The dialogue that follows the healing brings out what the "sign" signifies.

The setting this time is Jerusalem, at a pool where lie "many invalids – blind, lame, and paralyzed" – waiting to enter the pool "when the water is stirred up," for (so they believed) that would bring healing. (A passage not in the best manuscripts [see NRSV footnote], printed as verse four in older translations, explains that the stirring of the waters was caused by an angel and that the first sick person to enter thereafter would be healed.) One of the invalids is a man "ill for thirty-eight years" and needing help to get into the pool; since he has no one to help him, others get there ahead of him whenever the waters stir. As a result, he has been waiting "a long time." Jesus tells him to stand up, pick up the mat on which he has been lying, and walk. He is healed immediately, the proof being that he is able to do just as Jesus says.

Before telling the man to get up and walk, however, Jesus asks him, "Do you want to be made well?" Whether one *wants* to get well is a crucial question in sickness and healing. Perhaps recovery seems impossible, and "wanting" to get well too much to hope for. A long, disabling illness becomes part of the sick person's identity and social situation – something he or she may at times unconsciously shrink from relinquishing in favor of healing and the changes and adjustments connected with an altered identity. Just this – altered identity – is a prominent theme in the Gospel of John. Inseparable from it is the issue of Jesus' identity and the question whether one indeed wants to change. The dialogue in chapter three between Jesus and Nicodemus (3:1–21) will serve to illustrate.

In the Johannine dialogues, outsiders – or insiders still not fully "in the know" (such as various of Jesus' followers) – function as "straight men" giving literalistic, flatfooted responses to Jesus' "insider talk." Nicodemus, playing this role here, opens with the commonplace that no one can do the *sēmeia* Jesus is doing apart from God's presence. Jesus counters, unexpectedly, that no one can perceive God reigning apart from being born *anōthen*. As the NRSV indicates with its translation "from above" and the footnote "anew," this is a play on the double meaning of *anōthen*, one of those Johannine puns that insiders are expected to "get" but outsiders do not. Accordingly, Nicodemus wonders how a grown person can re-enter the womb and be born anew, or how what Jesus then says about birth *anōthen* through "water and spirit" is

possible. Jesus then reveals his identity, the identity Nicodemus had failed to perceive: he is the one "descended from
heaven," that is, "from above," and, like the bronze serpent
Moses "lifted up" to heal the Israelites bitten by poisonous
snakes (Num. 21:4–9), he too will be "lifted up," offering, here
and now, "eternal life" to those who believe in him (3:13–14;
cf. 3:31). Rebirth, then, is "from above," through Jesus, the one
from above, and the healing he offers is thus a healing not just
of physical ailments but of the whole person.

Such healing seems to be implied in the sequel to the
healing of the man at the pool, when Jesus tells him, "See,
you have been made well! Do not sin any more, so that
nothing worse happens to you" (5:14). In the healing story we
will examine next, Jesus rejects a causal connection between
sin and sickness (9:1–3). However, a passage like the present
one, or the forgiveness announced as part of the healing of the
paralyzed man in the Synoptics (see chapter 2 above), suggests
that sickness cannot easily be divided between "physical"
and "spiritual," between "outer self" and "inner self" (see,
further, chapter 8 below). This becomes evident in the long
discourse by Jesus that here follows the healing of the man at
the pool.

It comes about when the religious authorities upbraid the
man for carrying his mat – and thus working – on the sabbath.
When they learn that he is doing so at Jesus' instruction and
that Jesus has, in fact, healed on the Sabbath, their opposition
is aroused (5:9–16). Jesus outrages them further, first by
alluding to Jewish tradition (attested in Philo, *On the Cher-
ubim* 86–90, *Allegorical Interpretation* 1.5–6; and in various
later rabbinic sources) that envisaged God as necessarily
working on the Sabbath to sustain creation and the moral
order, and, second, by implying that in healing on the Sabbath
he was doing the work of "my Father" – "thereby making
himself equal to God" (5:17–18). That is, in healing and

bestowing life on the sabbath, Jesus, like his Father, is doing legitimate work (5:21).

Life is commonly regarded as the greatest gift, both to receive or to give (see 15:13). The life Jesus offers, however, is not this ordinary variety, the life that comes through human will (1:13) or means (3:4) and is dogged by sickness and haunted by death. Such life differs both in duration and in kind from the life Jesus offers. The adjective *aiōnios* prefaced to "life" in the Gospel of John expresses both aspects.

The life of which Jesus speaks will be, first, "eternal" (the usual translation of the Johannine *aiōnios*), that is, without end – persisting beyond death (5:28–29; 11:26). But, second, it begins even now (5:24–25), as a life different in kind from the life one is born into, as a life partaking of the new *aiōn*, the new age. The vision of a new age appeared in Judaism in the centuries immediately prior to the time of Jesus, in the literature called "apocalyptic" born of a longing for relief from oppression. (The Book of Daniel and the Book of Revelation, or the Apocalypse, are among the biblical examples.) What apocalyptic literature envisages as a new age on a cosmic scale the Gospel of John presents as a present possibility for the individual.

There are various ways in which the evangelist indicates how the possibility may be realized. In the dialogue with Nicodemus it is through "water and spirit" (3:5) and through believing in Jesus (3:15–16). In the long dialogue that follows the feeding of the multitude in chapter six, it is by eating "the bread from heaven," which is Jesus, "the bread of life" (6:32–35). Jesus tells those he has fed to "work" (*ergazesthe*) for such bread (6:27); at the same time it is a divine gift, as his feeding them signifies, a work (*ergon*) that God does, enabling recipients to believe in Jesus as sent by God (6:29). At the Festival of Booths, in chapter seven, Jesus proclaims that one receives life through drinking "living water," which the evangelist interprets as the giving of the Spirit after Jesus is glorified (7:37–39). At that time the Father will give the Spirit/ Advocate, who will bestow on the recipients understanding of who Jesus is and of his *sēmeia* (14:16, 26; 15:26; 16:13–14; cf. 2:18–22; 12:16).

These various statements presuppose, and sometimes refer to, the crucifixion and resurrection of Jesus, for John, like all the gospels, is a post-resurrection document, written after Jesus has (in Johannine terminology) been "lifted up" (3:14; 8:28; 12:32–34) and "glorified" (7:37–39; 12:16, 23), that is, after he is crucified and rises from the dead. Thus while we observe the earthly Jesus speaking to the people of his day, as readers we are expected to hear the risen Jesus speaking to us through the earthly Jesus, imparting insider information of a kind that invites and challenges us to make our own decisions about Jesus' identity and thus our own identity – whether we will want to be healed, to open ourselves to having life "abundantly" (10:10).

The man at the pool makes no direct response to Jesus' question whether he wants to be healed. Like many of us when we are sick, he knows and is fixated on only one mode of healing – in his case, entering the pool when the water is stirred (5:7), that is, at the time when the healing power was thought to be at work – and so he does not seem to hear Jesus' question. After he is healed he does not even know who healed him, for Jesus melts away into the crowd (5:11–13), and he learns who it is only because Jesus later seeks him out (5:14). Even then, all he knows is Jesus' name, which he reports to the authorities (5:15). The evangelist offers no criticism of him for not coming to the greater knowledge of Jesus that would bring him greater healing. What he has suffices for him, and he passes off the stage. Nonetheless, he stands in contrast to the protagonists in the next two healing *sēmeia*, who do indeed come to that fuller, healing mode of knowing Jesus.

Healing: believing is seeing

The account of the healing of a man blind from birth (9:1–41) begins with a question touched upon earlier in this book, the relation between sin and sickness. "Rabbi," ask Jesus' disciples, "who sinned, this man or his parents, that he was born blind?" Most modern readers would be relieved when they hear Jesus reply: "Neither." The rest of his reply, however, is, if anything, even more troubling to modern ears than if he had attributed the blindness to either the man or his parents: "he was born blind so that God's works might be revealed in him." Does God really intend evil in order to bring good out of it?

In our discussion of the healing of the paralyzed man in chapter 2, we saw that the Bible can ascribe both sickness and healing to God but that various passages seek to mitigate the starkness of that view. In other passages God is seen as directing the course of events to conform to the divine purpose (e.g., Gen. 50:15–20; Exod. 9:16; Rom. 9:17). This conviction is evident also in the Gospel of John, beginning in the very first chapter and repeatedly thereafter. As a consequence, like scenes in a movie that "dissolve" into one another, the purpose of Jesus' ministry, on the one hand, and the results of that ministry, on the other, tend to blend into one another, as here in Jesus' reply to his disciples' query. The same happens again in verse 39, and, as we shall see later, in chapter twelve, verses 37–40, which allude to or cite Hebrew prophets who, frustrated by rejection of their message, interpret this disappointing result as divine purpose – that is, what God had intended all along.

The way in which God's purpose will be revealed (9:3) in the *sēmeion* in chapter nine is specified, in "shorthand," in the next two verses (9:4–5). Jesus, who has been announced earlier as "the true light" (1:9) and as "the light of the world" (8:12), is here once again proclaimed as that light. In the "sign" that follows, we see how Jesus brings light to a man in darkness while on those unsympathetic to such enlightenment darkness descends. The blind man "sees" – both with his physical eyes and with the eyes of faith – whereas they remain "blind." The "sign" points to Jesus as the light and the Messiah: the blind man sees its significance, they do not.

The healing itself is markedly condensed (9:6–7): Jesus spits on the ground to make mud, spreads it on the man's eyes, and tells him, "Go, wash in the pool of Siloam." After doing so, he is able to see. There follows a series of interrogations in which the man gradually comes to "see" who Jesus is, while the interrogators' eye for who Jesus is grows increasingly dim. A summary cannot do justice to these artfully constructed dialogues, as readers of the biblical text will see for themselves.

The first set of interrogations (9:8–12) is essentially a series of puzzlements: is this really "the man who used to sit and beg?" Some say "yes," others, "no, it's someone who looks like him." He insists he is the man, and has to explain how he was healed. The scene closes with the man declaring he doesn't know who healed him – that has yet to be revealed to him.

He is then brought to the religious authorities (9:13–17), to whom he again has to explain how he received his sight. When they learn it was through mud made on the Sabbath – that is, work was performed – their ranks split: some say that someone who disregards the Sabbath cannot be from God; but "Wait," say others, "the working of such signs must surely show he is *not* a sinner." So the authorities ask the man his opinion, for "It was your eyes he opened." His response shows that his eyes are gradually being opened wider, for he now declares the unknown healer to be "a prophet."

The next scene (9:18–23) shows the authorities trying now to prove that the man had in fact never been blind, but then failing in their effort to do so. They ask his parents if he is indeed their son, born blind, and if so, how it is he now sees. They answer "yes" to the first question but dodge the second, professing ignorance and saying, "Ask him, he is of age. He will speak for himself." Their wariness is explained by the narrator as rooted in fear of being excluded from the synagogue if they "confessed Jesus to be the Messiah" (see further below). With this oblique reference to Jesus as Messiah, the scene closes.

So the authorities turn again to the son (9:24–34), in a most peremptory manner. "Give glory to God!" they admonish him. "We know that this man is a sinner." His answer is empirical: "Whether he is a sinner I don't know. One thing I do know: I was blind and now I see." When they keep quizzing him about the technique Jesus had employed, he retorts that he has already told them and they wouldn't listen, so "Why do you want to hear it again? Do you also want to become his disciples?" This ironic jab evokes a fierce response: "You're his disciple, but we are Moses' disciples. God spoke to Moses, but where 'this man' comes from we know not." This profession of ignorance is, as we saw earlier, a tacit, here ironic and unwitting acknowledgment that Jesus is indeed the Messiah.

The man's rejoinder is a masterpiece of rhetoric and logic. He professes astonishment at the authorities' ignorance. You don't know whence he comes (whether from God, or not) – "yet he opened my eyes." You call him a sinner – yet God listens to those, sinners included, who worship him and do his will, and God must certainly be listening to this man, the proof being that he did the absolutely unheard of: he "opened the eyes of a person born blind." The empirical and theological evidence is all on the side of the man. The only rejoinder the authorities can muster is, first, to vilify him by resort to a theological commonplace that Jesus has earlier rejected – being born blind shows "You were born entirely in sin" – and then to humiliate him: You, a sinner, are trying to teach us – ?! Backed

into a rhetorical corner, their final tactic is to drive him from
their presence. The upshot is that they have now completely
closed their eyes to the possibility that Jesus is from God,
while the man now sees clearly that Jesus must indeed be from
God.

The final scene (9:35–41) is the climax. Jesus reappears, and
through him the man's ever expanding vision is brought to full
sight while the authorities' blindness is pronounced complete.
Jesus, hearing of the man's expulsion, seeks him out and
reveals that he is the Son of Man (cf. 1:51). The man responds,
"Lord, I believe," falls on his face, and worships Jesus, the
appropriate response to divine self-disclosure (see Gen. 17:3;
Lev. 9:24; Josh. 5:14; Matt. 17:6; Luke 5:8; Rev. 1:17; 11:16;
19:10). On the other hand those who do not see what this
"sign" of restoration of sight signifies – Jesus as light – are
blind.

In the other gospels, a blind man healed is restored to full
participation in society. That is part of his healing, and another
aspect of Jesus' healing, as was indicated in the preceding
chapters. Here the opposite happens: the man is excluded from
his accustomed community, and his parents fear to be
excluded also, through association with him and, through him,
with Jesus. Though the story is set in the time of Jesus, this
aspect of the *sēmeion* reflects the time of the evangelist
toward the end of the first century CE when the split between
synagogue and church had gone far and Jews confessing Jesus
as Messiah felt compelled, at least in the evangelist's milieu,
to do so furtively (see 3:1–2; 12:42; 16:2–4; cf. 7:13 and 19:38).
The hostility of the religious authorities to Jesus in the gospel
reflects in part antagonism between Jesus and Jewish authorities in his day; but the evangelist's black-and-white portrayal
of the hostility of Jesus' opponents, and his stereotyping of
them ("*the* Jews," "*the* Pharisees"), reflect even more the
antagonism between the evangelist's community and the Jews

of his day who did not acknowledge Jesus as Messiah. Those Jews who publicly confess Jesus as Messiah and face exclusion from the Jewish community must thus seek their home instead in the evangelist's community. There they will find the life and light that make whole as Jesus seeks and finds them, just as he once sought out and found the man in our story.

To that community Jesus promises that once he has returned to the Father the members will do the works he did and, indeed, "greater works than these" (14:12). Today, in whatever Christian communities succeeded that community, one of those works would be to heal the millennia-long rift between Jews and Christians occasioned in part by the sort of uncritical reading of the Gospel of Matthew (see chapter 3 above) and the Gospel of John that sees in the stereotyped, negative renderings of Jews in those gospels an adequate, accurate portrait of Jews then or since. Such "seeing" is a form of blindness.

Jesus prefaces the *sēmeion* in chapter nine with a note of urgency: "We must work the works of him who sent me while it is day; night is coming when no one can work" (9:4). This is another distinctively Johannine way in which Jesus predicts his suffering and death (cf. 13:30), when the powerful worker of *sēmeia* will be powerless – though his giving himself over into the power of others is viewed as a deliberate act within his power (10:17–18). Before that happens, he will exercise his power in the last (and most spectacular) *sēmeion* of all, the raising of Lazarus from the dead, which in turn leads to Jesus' own death.

The ultimate healing

The evangelist links this final healing *sēmeion* in the gospel (11:1–53) to the preceding one in several ways. First, early on, he provides a shorthand statement of the significance of the sign: both Lazarus' illness (11:4) and the beggar's blindness (9:3) are to serve God's purposes. (What was said there about the blending of divine purpose and result would apply here as well.) Second, in both accounts Jesus strikes a note of urgency in his statements about taking advantage of the daylight (9:4; 11:9–10). Third, the mourners at Lazarus' tomb know of Jesus' healing of the blind man and ask whether he could not also have healed Lazarus (11:37). Fourth, implicit in this question is the significance of each sign: in opening the eyes of the blind man Jesus showed he was light; in healing Lazarus of the ultimate sickness, death, and in giving him the ultimate gift, life, Jesus shows he is life. The two *sēmeia* together thus exemplify the assertion in the Prologue to the gospel that Jesus is both life and light (1:4). Finally, the irony and plays on words in chapter nine ("seeing," "blindness") appear here again, in abundance.

The word-plays in chapter eleven have to do with death and life. Lazarus' sisters, Mary and Martha, send word to Jesus from their home in Bethany that he is ill, in the expectation (see 11:21, 32) that Jesus will come and heal him; but Jesus deliberately delays going to him (11:1–6). He asserts that "this illness does not lead to death" (11:4) – a puzzling assertion in view of the later report that Lazarus does indeed die. It is the first of the word-plays on "death," raising the question of what is meant by "death." A bit later, Jesus tells his disciples that Lazarus "has fallen asleep" and "I am going there to awaken him" (11:11). The disciples, the "straight men" in this dialogue, surmise, not surprisingly, that Lazarus' sleep is good news, a sign of recovery, and that therefore "he will be all right" (11:12). The evangelist then explains to the reader that by "sleep" Jesus meant "death" (11:13). But the subsequent narrative will reveal that it is indeed a "sleep," from which Jesus will "awaken" him.

When Jesus arrives in Bethany another dialogue ensues, this

time with Martha (11:17–27). Lazarus has now been dead four days. Martha expresses her belief that had Jesus arrived earlier he could have been healed. She is further confident that "even now" God would undo the death were Jesus to ask it. Then, as in the dialogue with Nicodemus, Jesus gives the conversation an unexpected turn: "Your brother will rise again." Martha gives a "straight" answer, namely, that, yes, Lazarus will participate in the general resurrection of the dead: "I know that he will rise again in the resurrection on the last day." Neither confirming nor denying this commonplace among Jews of the time (see Dan. 12:2; 2 *Maccabees* 7:9, 14, 23, 29; cf. Mark 12:18; Acts 23:8), Jesus instead adds another dimension to it: "resurrection" is not only a promise for the future, it is a possibility right now in the present. This is because he is "the resurrection and the life." From this premise proceed two, inextricably linked possibilities mentioned for those who believe in him as "the resurrection and the life." One is that "even though they die, they will live" (11:25). That is, physical death is inevitable, to be sure, but the believer will live beyond death. The maxim Jesus applies to his own death later on applies to his followers' deaths as well: a grain of wheat is capable of life only if it "falls into the earth and dies" (12:24; cf. 1 Cor. 15:35–56). The second possibility is that those who are now living and believing in Jesus will never die at all (11:26): they will pass from life (in the old *aiōn*) to life (in the new *aiōn*), undergoing the change in identity mentioned earlier in this chapter as a healing of the whole person.

There we saw that Jesus as the one "from above" laid out the possibility of such change to Nicodemus, concluding with an anticipation of the promise made here to Martha and (as a counterpart) of the judgment on those who spurn the promise: those who believe in the Son have the life of the new *aiōn* whereas those who do not "will not see life" (3:36). In the two *sēmeia* in chapters four and five of the gospel Jesus showed

himself to be the giver of life, leading up to statements that
anticipate the possibilities Jesus holds out in speaking to
Martha. Those who hear Jesus and believe the One who sent
him *have* the life of the new *aiōn* and have "passed from death
[the old *aiōn*] to life" (5:24). That hour "is coming, and is now
here" (5:25). That present life also looks to the future life: "the
hour is coming when all who are in their graves will hear his
[the Son of Man's] voice and will come out" – either to "the
resurrection of life" or to "the resurrection of condemnation"
(5:28–29). This promise of resurrection is then repeated by
Jesus (6:40, 54) in the sequel to the *sēmeion* of the feeding of
the multitude (6:1–14).

Readers of the gospel may thus perhaps be expected to be
prepared for Jesus' promises to Martha. As for Martha, she is –
and she isn't. When asked by Jesus if she believes them (11:26)
she responds with the Johannine counterpart to Peter's confession at Caesarea Philippi (Mark 8:29//Matt 16:16, Luke 9:20):
"I believe that you are the Messiah, the Son of God, the one
coming into the world" (11:27). Again she is reciting Jewish
tradition, applying it now to Jesus; but that she believes in him
as "the resurrection and the life" does not yet seem to be part
of her credo, for later, when Jesus commands that the stone be
removed from her brother's tomb, she is aghast, protesting that
Lazarus' four-day-old corpse will be giving off a stench (11:39).
Resurrection and life are out of the question. Martha – but
Martha as representing the readers as well – will need the
sēmeion itself – Jesus demonstrating he is indeed "the resurrection and the life" by raising her brother – to become convinced
of that.

To Jesus' promises about resurrection and life the evangelist
adds further preparation for the *sēmeion*: the emotions sur-
rounding death. People have come to console Martha and Mary
(11:19, 31); Mary and her comforters weep (11:33); and Jesus
joins in (11:35). He has other reactions as well. He is "deeply

moved" and he is angered (*enebrimēsato*) (11:33). The NRSV translates *enebrimēsato* as "greatly disturbed," and so he was; but other occurrences of the word (Dan. 11:30 in one Greek translation of the Hebrew; Mark 14:5) suggest that "angered" may be a more adequate rendering here. As we saw in chapter 2, Jesus, faced with sickness, seems to have been angered, as though by a hostile power (Mark 1:41, NRSV note; Luke 4:39). Confronted with death, a manifestation of Satan's power, Jesus is angered. (One may recall that therapists today may counsel patients to acknowledge and give expression in some way to their anger over sickness or death.)

The *sēmeion* itself is tersely narrated. Jesus commands the stone to be taken away from the tomb; Martha objects; Jesus counters her objection, and then, having prayed, in a loud voice summons Lazarus forth, whereupon he emerges in his grave cloths. At Jesus' command these are removed and he is "let go" (11:38–44).

The reaction to the *sēmeion* is twofold (11:45–53): some believe in Jesus, a response that moves the religious authorities to plot Jesus' death because his "many signs" are attracting so many followers that he poses a religious and political threat to the status quo. The high priest proposes a common-sense expedient: better that one person die for the people than that a whole people should be destroyed. In the Johannine context this is an ironic utterance, a double-edged statement: for the evangelist, and for early Christian tradition generally, Jesus does indeed die for others, giving his life for their salvation.

The words "glory" and "glorified" in the mouth of Jesus are also double-edged and recall the treatment of Jesus' healings in the Gospel of Mark (chapter 2 above). There we saw that to interpret Jesus' messiahship with reference only to the power manifested in the healings and other miracles is to misinterpret it. Only when it is clear that he must, as Messiah, suffer and die does Jesus acknowledge messiahship. In the Gospel of

John, when one hears the word "glory" one expects wonder and power. And one is not disappointed. We learn that Jesus' turning water into wine, the first *sēmeion*, "revealed his glory" (2:11). Likewise, the final *sēmeion*, the raising of Lazarus, is "for God's glory," to glorify the Son (11:4), and when Martha sees Lazarus coming forth she will be beholding "the glory of God" (11:40). But that manifestation of glory leads to another unexpected kind of glory, Jesus' (ironic) exaltation – on a cross, on which he is lifted up (3:14; 8:28; 12:32–33) – and which together with his rising from the dead constitute the "hour" that "glorifies" the Son and the Father (17:1, 5). This is the ultimate victory over death, the ultimate "healing," "the resurrection and the life." Thus the first, creating Word (1:1–4) is also the final Word who (to borrow the phraseology of Second Maccabees) "will in his mercy give life and breath back to you" after death (2 *Macc.* 7:23).

Healing: believing without seeing

A postscript to the final healing *sēmeion* reports that the "many signs" Jesus had performed met with disbelief on the part of those who witnessed them. The evangelist portrays this reaction as fulfilling a Hebrew prophet's lament about rejection of his message (John 12:37–38, citing Isa. 53:1). As a result, the healing the Lord sought to offer the prophet's hearers they did not receive (John 12:39–40, citing Isa. 6:9–10).

The readers of the gospel, unlike the characters in the Gospel of John, are not "there" to observe first-hand the healing *sēmeia* and Jesus who performed them. Nor can they, like Thomas, verify that Jesus has indeed conquered by feeling his wounded hands and side (20:24–28). However, to the same readers the Johannine Jesus delivers a message. Thomas believed because he saw. But "Blessed are those who have not seen and yet have come to believe" (20:29). The evangelist adds that of the many "signs" Jesus did, he has recorded the ones he has so that "you [readers] may come to believe that Jesus is the Messiah, the Son of God, and that through believing you may have life in his name" (20:30–31).

Chapter 7 will examine how Jesus' early followers offered life and healing "in his name." The final chapter will stand aside from the New Testament gospels, and the accounts of healing by his followers, and ask whether Jesus did really heal. First, however, a brief look at Jesus as healer in a few early Christian sources outside the New Testament.

Chapter 6

Jesus as Healer: Apocryphal Writings

The Gospel of John concludes with the observation that Jesus did many things not recorded in the gospel and that, if they were, probably "the world itself could not contain the books that would be written" (21:25). The New Testament gospels represent only a small selection of the many gospels and other writings produced by early Christians subsequent, in most cases, to the composition of the New Testament writings. These later works are called non-canonical (because they were not included in the New Testament canon) or apocryphal, which means "secret" or "hidden" but came to be used to designate writings excluded from the Bible. They demonstrate that the portraits of Jesus as healer in the New Testament are part of a larger early Christian picture of Jesus as healer, as a few examples will show.

Recapitulations

Some of the apocryphal writings add little to the New Testament picture of Jesus as healer. They recapitulate, with some differences, what is found in the New Testament. For example, the very fragmentary gospel (some two papyrus leaves) known as the Egerton Papyrus and dated to the early second century CE offers another version of the Synoptic account of a healing of a leper (Mark 1:40–45//Matt. 8:1–4, Luke 5:12–16). A leper approaches Jesus, tells him he has become infected by eating with lepers in an inn, and asks to be cleansed; Jesus heals him and tells him to show himself to the priests. While there is some evidence that the papyrus records early tradition, this passage shows ignorance of the Holy Land in the first-century. Lepers did not stay in inns; they were kept at a distance because they were considered "unclean" (see Num. 12:15; 2 Kings 7:3–4). Moreover, a cleansed leper went to a priest, not to "the priests," to obtain certification of the cleansing.

The *Epistle of the Apostles*, a second-century CE writing that purports to be a letter from the eleven remaining apostles, mentions several of Jesus' healing miracles and gives shortened versions of the healing of the Gadarene/Gerasene demoniac and of the hemorrhaging woman. In the *Acts of Pilate* (likely dateable as early as the second century CE) the same woman emerges from the anonymity of the New Testament account, and we learn her name is Bernice or Veronica (*Acts of Pilate* 7). Individuals we have encountered in the preceding chapters appear in another passage in the *Acts* (6.1–2) in which each tells Pontius Pilate how they were healed: the paralyzed man (Mark 2:1–12//Matt. 9:1–8, Luke 5:17–26) and the man who was an invalid for thirty-eight years (John 5:1–9), these two persons here telescoped into one; the blind man in John (9:1–41) and in the Synoptics (Mark 10:46–52//Luke 18:35–43), again regarded as one and the same; a leper (Mark 1:40–44//Matt. 8:1–4, Luke 5:12–16); and the woman (here turned into a man) unable to straighten herself (Luke 13:10–13). Another passage attests Jesus' power over demons and his raising of Lazarus (John 11) – reports of which cause Pilate to tremble (*Acts of Pilate* 8).

Passages such as these would serve to enhance Jesus' reputation as healer. In the *Acts of Pilate* even the Roman official responsible for Jesus' death (though the blame is here put on the Jews) is presented as learning of Jesus' wondrous healings – information wholly absent from the New Testament. It is evident that the New Testament accounts of Jesus' healings did not act as a brake on the elaboration of these traditions by subsequent generations of his followers. Indeed, they seem to have inspired it, for the apocryphal supplements to the canonical portrayals of Jesus as healer help to satisfy some of the curiosity that the New Testament accounts often arouse. They also reinforce the New Testament picture of Jesus as compassionate.

Jesus as superboy healer

A quite different picture emerges, however, in the *Infancy Gospel of Thomas*, also dating to the second century. Here Jesus the miracle-worker of the New Testament gospels is seen working miracles already as a child. Some of these are such that any child might wish to perform (for example, turning clay birds into actual sparrows; 2.1–5). Other miracles assist his mother with chores (11.1–2) and his father in his carpentry (13.1–2). A number of times he performs healings (9.1–3; 10.1–2; 16.1–2; 17.1–2; 18.1–2). At other times, however, persons who offend Jesus in some way incur his curse and die (3–5; 14.2), so that no one dares to provoke him (8.2; 14.3). Such narratives tell readers more about Jesus' (supposed) boyhood than they probably care to know. Jesus emerges not only as a compassionate healer but also as quick-tempered and vengeful, working hurt, not healing.

Jesus as "useful" healer

A fourth-century document that scholars have entitled *The Legend of Abgar* purports to record correspondence between Jesus and Abgar, king of Edessa (modern Urfa in eastern Turkey). Abgar writes that he has heard of Jesus' healings and begs Jesus to come and heal him of the affliction he is suffering. In his reply Jesus blesses Abgar for believing without seeing (cf. John 20:29) and explains (in Johannine language) that he is unable to come because he must carry out his earthly mission. However, after he is "taken up," he will send a disciple to heal Abgar and bring life to him and the Edessans. This disciple turns out to be the apostle Thaddaeus, who heals the king by laying his hand on him in the name of Jesus. This and other healings lead to proclamation of the Christian message to the populace and thus to "the life" Jesus promised Abgar.

Scholars are generally agreed that this account represents an effort to conceal the true origins of Edessan Christianity, which owed its inception to varieties of Christianity that came to be viewed with disfavor by the Christian authorities in fourth-century Edessa. One sees, then, how Jesus' reputation as healer has been put to use in producing the document. The supposed correspondence, recorded on papyri, ostraca, or stone, also came to function as a talisman against sickness and other misfortunes. Similar talismans from roughly the same period have been found preserved in the dry sands of Egypt. Worn as amulets, they record summaries of Jesus' healing activity (Matt. 4:23–24) or other New Testament verses. Like Abgar, the wearers had not seen Jesus but yet believed in his power to heal and protect them from harm.

It is evident from this sampling of apocrypha that the image of Jesus as healer in the New Testament gospels exercised a powerful influence upon subsequent generations of his followers. Indeed, these same followers testified that, through them, Jesus continued to heal, as we see in the next chapter.

Chapter 7

"In His Name": Jesus Heals Through His Followers

In all four New Testament gospels, as we have seen, Jesus sends his followers out to heal. However, only the Gospel of Luke has a direct sequel – the Acts of the Apostles – that shows them doing so. But there are numerous other Christian sources, beginning with the letters of Paul and continuing on into the Middle Ages, that constitute indirect sequels to Jesus' healings in the New Testament gospels – responses, as it were, to the charge given to his earliest followers. These various sources make clear that early Christians viewed his healings as set forth in the gospels not as once-for-all manifestations of God's power and life, but as something continuing, and to be continued. In the ancient Mediterranean world where, as we observed in chapter 1, life was precarious and good health highly prized, persons offering healing would be welcomed by many.

In his book *Christianizing the Roman Empire* (1984), Yale University historian Ramsay MacMullen contends that it was in fact Christian miracles, including healings, more than any other factor that won converts. Especially crucial, according to early Christian testimony, was the expulsion of demons, or as moderns might be inclined to say, the healing of mental illness, which in ancient paganism ranked much lower on the healing scale than did bodily ailments. For Jesus' followers, however, the driving out of demons was a dramatic demonstration of the superiority of the Christian God over the demons and deities of paganism. Various early Christian writers tout it as a distinctive mark of Christianity and as a means of winning converts. Thus, around the middle of the second century CE Justin Martyr boasts that Christians cast out demons by reciting a little credo about Jesus' crucifixion (2 Apology 6.6; similarly, Justin's Dialogue with Trypho 30.3; 76.7; 85.2–3) – an interesting early example of how the story of the powerless healer begins to be used as a power for healing in his name. A few decades later, Irenaeus, bishop of Lyons, reports that those from whom demons have been expelled are frequently won to Christ (Against Heresies 2.33.4). Tertullian, a couple of decades further still (197 CE), asserts that evil spirits inhabiting humans or masquerading as deities reveal their true identities when a follower of Christ orders them to speak (Apol. 23.4).

The stories of Jesus as healer that have been the subject of the preceding chapters were themselves also a significant factor in winning persons to Christianity. As was observed in chapters 1 and 2, healing stories were not uncommon in pagan antiquity, and many pagans evidently found that the Christian variety of healings raised the hope that as this Jesus had once healed the sick in Galilee and Judea, so he might perhaps heal them too, in Syria or Greece or Italy. One can understand, then, why early Christians would want to preserve and eventually record stories of Jesus as healer, whether in the New Testament gospels or in other writings. The stories were useful both in missionary proclamation and as a basis and confirmation of Christian healing: hear how Jesus healed; and, we, as his followers, now do the same. This chapter looks at some examples.

Paul: signs and wonders, but . . .

Though the letters of Paul follow the gospels in the New Testament, they precede the gospels in time of writing. Paul's letters are thus the earliest Christian documents we possess, dating to the fifties of the first century CE, and it is appropriate to begin with them. From one of his letters to the Christian community in Corinth, we learn that some members are practicing healing. Paul calls healing a "gift" given by God's Spirit to those for whom "Jesus is Lord" (1 Cor. 12:3); he lists it (12:9, 28, 30) as one of a number of gifts bestowed by the Spirit.

Paul himself was not one of those original followers of Jesus whom the New Testament calls "apostles," and his claim to be an apostle came under attack. One of the ways he defended himself was to offer as "signs [sēmeia] of a true apostle" the "signs [sēmeia] and wonders and mighty works" he performed in Corinth (2 Cor. 12:12). This evidently took place on his first coming to Corinth, as a reinforcement of his missionary message and as a means of winning converts. This approach is in fact indicated in Paul's letter to the Romans: Christ worked "through me to win obedience [i.e., faith; see Rom. 1:5] from the Gentiles by word *and deed*, by the power of *signs and wonders*, by the power of the Spirit of God" (Rom. 15:18–19, emphasis added; similarly, 1 Thess. 4:5). For reasons to be given later (see chapter 8), healings would seem the most likely "sign" or "wonder" denoted by Paul with the stock biblical phrase "signs and wonders" (see Exod. 7:3; Deut. 4:34, 6:22; 26:8; 29:3; 34:11; Neh. 9:10; Isa. 8:18; Jer. 32:20, 21; Dan. 4:2; John 4:48; Acts 2:22, 43; 5:12; 7:36; 14:3; 15:12; 2 Thess. 2:9; Heb. 2:4).

Outweighing this kind of "powerful" defense of his apostleship are those passages in which Paul recites as demonstrations of his apostleship just the opposite, the sufferings he endured as an apostle (1 Cor. 4:11–18; 2 Cor. 6:3–10; 11:23–27). If Paul was a healer, then, like the physician in the proverb mentioned earlier, he was unable to heal himself. And praying to Christ for healing, he was refused and told that it was precisely in his weakness that Christ's power was manifested (2 Cor. 12:7–10;

cf. 1 Cor. 4:9–10; 2 Cor. 4:7–12). Such an interpretation of his sickness accords with the story of the crucified healer that concludes each of the gospels. That Paul is thus able to come to terms with his persisting illness is, as a healer or psychotherapist today might say, itself a form of healing. By contrast, in the Acts of the Apostles the picture of Paul as healer, as well as of the other apostles, is that of a worker of "signs and wonders."

Acts of the Apostles: in the name of Jesus

Paul, the wounded healer of his letters, appears in the Acts of the Apostles as an invulnerable healer: when a deadly snake fastens itself to Paul's hand, he simply shakes it off, with no ill effects (28:1–6). However, before he ever does any healing – of himself or others – he must himself be healed, in his case of the blindness resulting from a vision of the risen Jesus; restored to health, Paul is then to bring the "name" of Jesus to others (9:1–18). "Bringing the name" included not only proclaiming the message about Jesus as deliverer from sin but also healing in his name.

In chapter 2 we saw that names possess and confer power – the power and indeed the presence of the bearer of the name. Thus in Acts Peter invokes the presence of Jesus simply by speaking his name: "Aeneas, Jesus Christ heals you" (9:34). When Peter, "in the name of Jesus Christ of Nazareth," heals a lame man, the response (as in the gospels) is "wonder and amazement" (3:1–10) but also opposition from the religious leaders, who think that by forbidding Peter and John to use the name of Jesus, they can squelch the budding Jesus movement (4:1–22). Later, we observe Paul silencing a spirit "in the name of Jesus" (16:16–18).

For the author of Acts, the name of Jesus does not function as a formula uttered at will to produce automatic healing.

Some Jewish exorcists who attempt to use it in this way to expel an evil spirit provoke a violent reaction instead: the possessed man, crying out, "Jesus I know, and Paul I know; but who are you?," leaps on them and drives them away (19:13–16). Nor can the Spirit be purchased (8:14–24). It is only the followers of Jesus who can heal in his name. It is only they whom he has empowered by the Holy Spirit (Luke 24:49; Acts 1:4; 2:1–4) – which is his Spirit (16:7) – even as he was himself empowered by the Spirit (chapter 4 above). The gift of the Spirit transforms dispirited, confused disciples (Luke 24) into bold proclaimers of the risen Jesus who win other followers – and provoke opposition – both by their message and by the healings and other miracles that accompany the message, all the way from Jerusalem to Rome (Acts 1:8; 28:30–31). In addition to the summary statements of healings in Acts (5:16; 8:6–7; 28:9), there are accounts of healings of various maladies that recall those in the Gospel of Luke (see Acts 3:1–16; 9:17–18, 32–34; 14:8–10; 16:16–18; 28:8). As in Luke, resurrections are also reported (9:36–42; 20:9–12).

In several respects, however, some of the healing accounts in Acts differ from those in Luke and anticipate later development of Christian healing traditions examined further on in this chapter. One difference is the spectacular, wondrous nature of certain accounts. People bring the sick into the streets where Peter will be walking and position them so that his shadow will fall on them and heal them (Acts 5:15). As evidence of "extraordinary miracles" wrought by God through Paul, the author says that "handkerchiefs and aprons that had touched his skin" heal the sick (16:12). Paul's invulnerability to deadly venom has already been mentioned.

Both Peter (3:12–16) and Paul (14:14–15) disclaim any healing powers apart from Jesus. But readers may forget those disclaimers when, page after page, they read of the many healings and other miracles performed by the two apostles and the power that emanates even from an object touched to them or from their mere shadow. Readers of the time familiar with traditions of, or encounters with, healers or others who emanate power (see chapter 2 above) might well begin to view apostles of Jesus as powerful in themselves, apart from Jesus. That begins to happen in the apocryphal acts (see below). Sheer wonder also assumes a larger role in those writings than one finds here in canonical Acts.

Another feature of certain of the miracles in the New Testament book of Acts is their punitive nature – they harm rather than heal. A couple who lie to Peter about money they have given to the common purse of the Christian community in Jerusalem are both struck dead (5:1–11). King Herod suffers the same fate for assuming divine honors (12:20–23). Even as Paul is temporarily blinded for opposing Jesus (9:3–9), so also a Jewish opponent of Paul is stricken with temporary blindness (13:6–11). Social and religious rivalries are evident in this account set on the island of Cyprus. The man is on good terms with the proconsul, the chief Roman official on the island, and fearing that the proconsul's embrace of the religion Paul is proclaiming may estrange the proconsul from himself, he seeks to turn him away from Christianity and from Paul, and is blinded as a result.

The author of Acts labels the man a "false prophet" and "magician." Such judgments are in the eye of the beholder and are influenced by group loyalties. In the next century we observe pagan opponents of Christianity beginning to claim that Jesus was a magician who performed wonders through magical arts (e.g., Celsus, *True Discourse*, in Origen, *Against Celsus* 1:6, 28, 71), a charge stoutly denied by Christians (e.g., Justin, 1 *Apology* 30). The same charge is laid against Jesus' follower, Judas Thomas, in the apocryphal *Acts of Thomas*, as we see next.

Acts of Thomas

In the Gospel of John, Thomas is called "the Twin" (Greek, *Didymos*; 11:16; 20:24; 21:2). "Thomas" itself also means "twin" (Aramaic, *T'ômâ*). In the *Acts of Thomas* (third century CE) he appears with the name Judas Thomas and as the twin of Jesus, who sends him to India in order to win it to Christianity. Healing is one of the means Thomas employs. In the name of Jesus, Thomas orders a snake to suck out the venom from a man it has bitten (30–33). A demon who has been plaguing a woman for five years leaves her when confronted by Thomas (42–46). A young man whose hands wither when he receives the eucharist because he has murdered his girlfriend is cured when he repents; she in turn is resurrected (51–54). Such spectacular healings appear in other apocryphal acts as well, foreshadowing similar displays in the medieval lives of the saints.

As in the New Testament gospels, so here too in the *Acts of Thomas* the healings serve larger purposes. In *Thomas* they lead to lives divorced from the material and the transitory and devoted instead to the spiritual and the eternal and to the ascetic practice deemed essential to these. In the case of women, such lives estrange them from their husbands, who in their frustration charge that Thomas is a magician and sorcerer (96, 98, 101, 102, 104, 106, 130, 152, 162) who has an evil eye (100) and casts spells on their wives. For the women, however, Thomas is a physician of the soul (95). The social discord sown by Christianity, also through healings (cf. Acts 16:16–24), is reflected in these stories.

Eventually some husbands, too, are won over, and at the conclusion of the *Acts* even the king, who has had Thomas put to death, turns to the apostle for help (170). Desperate because his son is possessed by a demon, the king comes to the apostle's tomb hoping to take one of his bones and fasten it to his son and thereby heal him. There Thomas appears to him, chiding him for believing in him when dead but not when living. Nonetheless, the apostle assures the king that Jesus will deal kindly with him. The king, on finding that Christians have stolen the body of Thomas, takes dust on which it has lain and applies it to his son, who then recovers. The king's actions reflect the common pagan belief that the tombs or remains of certain renowned individuals known as "heroes" exert power. It was a belief that persisted into medieval Christianity where it was thought the remains ("relics") of heroes of faith in Jesus – the martyrs and saints – could also bring healing to the sick.

Chapter 8

Did Jesus Really Heal?

Posing the questions

Persons in the Western world who have never picked up a Bible are nonetheless apt to have at least a nodding acquaintance with various stories from the Bible – Adam and Eve, Noah and the ark, David and Goliath, the Good Samaritan, the Prodigal Son. Children used to grow up with Bible story books; those stories are still the staple of much Sunday school instruction. The spells stories cast is not limited to children. How many adults can resist the line, "Once upon a time," or the standup comic's "On the way over here I ran into ...," or "Then some people came, bringing to him a paralyzed man"? Had most of what we know about Jesus as healer come in the form of sermon or learned treatise, it is unlikely that the image of him as caring and compassionate – and healing – would have exercised the influence it has upon subsequent generations.

Those stories are, however, parts of larger stories, the New Testament gospels. These, too, have had a profound influence, not only in the Western world (one thinks of Gandhi, for example) and not only on believers, for whom these stories were "good news," but also on persons who had little time for Christianity but yet found much to admire in the gospels' portraits of Jesus. In the modern period, however, many believers and non-believers alike began to ask whether those portraits were trustworthy. For well over two centuries now scholars have been sifting through the Jesus traditions in the New Testament gospels and other early Christian writings in an attempt to discern there "the historical Jesus": Jesus as a modern historian might describe him using the canons and criteria of history the way it began to be written in the modern period and especially in the nineteenth century. This investigation has intensified in recent years as scholars have refined historical method, drawing upon scholarship in fields such as sociology and anthropology. The "quest for the historical Jesus" (as it came to be called) went hand in hand with efforts to discover how the gospels came to be, whether one gospel writer used the other(s), what other sources each might have employed. The evangelists were seen as collectors and assemblers of traditions, "scissors-and-paste" people, so to speak.

In their eager pursuit of answers to these questions, however, scholars tended to lose sight of the gospels as works of imagination as well as inspiration (in whatever sense) – aesthetic entities, not mere collages of fragments. In recent decades, however, scholars have developed new respect for the evangelists as authors and for the gospels as stories, with much material common to all four and yet each distinct from the other and with many layers of meaning. It is this approach to the gospels that is represented in the preceding chapters. It was a principle of method to seek to let the gospel writers address readers on the writers' own terms.

One hopes thus to skirt "the peril of modernizing Jesus" mentioned in chapter 2. At the same time, however, one courts the opposite danger of "playing first-century Bible land" (as one scholar has put it) – the notion that through diligent research we can somehow live our way back into the time of Jesus. However, we are, and remain, children of the twentieth century, soon (barring nuclear holocausts or meltdowns or other catastrophes) of the twenty-first. As much as we may appreciate the art of the gospel writers and perhaps, along with millions of others in the past two millennia, receive as "good news" the portraits those writers have left to us of Jesus – and of Jesus as healer – yet we live in what the famous German sociologist Max Weber called a "disenchanted" world. The questions we may raise about the healings supposedly performed before our eyes on the television screen we may be inclined to pose also to the gospel accounts of Jesus' healings, where any answers may be even more difficult to come by. Not only are the evangelist's descriptions of the illnesses scanty and the terminology difficult to correlate with present-day medical language, but no first-hand examination of "before" and "after" is possible across the twenty centuries that separate us from the supposed healings.

What kind of answers can one expect when one asks, "Did Jesus really heal?" Here it is well to keep in mind that answers to historical questions such as this range from impossibility to possibility to probability to certainty. We are certain that John F. Kennedy was shot on November 22, 1963. The official investigation by the Warren Commission concluded that shots were fired by one person situated on the sixth floor of the Texas School Book Depository. A virtual industry of dissent sees that as one possibility, or even probability, but certainly not as certain. If an event so recent is so disputed, how much more is one constrained to speak of possibilities and probabilities when studying persons and events of 2,000 years ago.

Though in the early years of this century it was fashionable in some circles to question whether Jesus ever lived, his existence is at least as certain as that of the emperor Augustus or Pontius Pilate or Philo of Alexandria or other such contemporaries of Jesus. The details of Jesus' life, however, are much less certain, and investigating what degree of possibility or probability or certainty to assign each has become something of a cottage industry for some New Testament scholars. One scholar prominent in this research, John Dominic Crossan, concludes in his exhaustive study, *The Historical Jesus* (1991), that miracle accounts belong to the earliest strata of Jesus traditions (pp. 310–11). Some years earlier, approaching the question from quite a different perspective, Morton Smith came to a similar conclusion: Jesus' popularity, and the opposition he aroused, are credible only if he was perceived by the populace as performing miracles (*Jesus the Magician*, 1978).

A close comparison of the healing accounts in a synopsis of the first three New Testament gospels will show they not infrequently diverge from one another, in detail if not necessarily in substance. Were there two blind men healed at Jericho (Matt. 20:30) or just one (Mark 10:46//Luke 18:35), and was the same man unidentifiable (Luke 18:35) or was he known to followers of Jesus as "Bartimaeus son of Timaeus" (Mark 10:46)? Was he (or they) healed as Jesus was leaving Jericho (Mark and Matthew) or on entering it (Luke)?

Were there two demoniacs healed (Matt. 8:28) or just one (Mark 5:2//Luke 8:27), and did it take place in the territory of the Gerasenes (Mark 5:1//Luke 8:26) or that of the Gadarenes (Matt. 8:28), thus (as was pointed out in chapter 3 above) reducing the distance the pigs had to run to the Sea of Galilee by about twenty-seven miles. Since Gadara is, however, still six miles from the Sea, it is understandable that some New Testament manuscripts read "Gergesa." According to Origen (c. 185–c. 254 CE), who resided for some time in the Holy Land, this locale was close to the Sea, with a cliff nearby down which the pigs could have run (Origen, *Commentary on John* 6.41).

Did a good number of Jesus' healings follow one after another (Matt. 8–9), or were these same healings dispersed over a period of time (as in Luke)? As was indicated in the chapter on Matthew, the grouping of healings in Matthew 8 and 9 is distinctively Matthean and, placed after the Sermon on the Mount, is the author's way of suggesting that Jesus is Messiah in deed (through healings) as well as in word (the Sermon on the Mount). These various examples illustrate further what was evident in the preceding chapters on healings in each of the four New Testament gospels: while the four share many of the same or similar healing traditions, they report them differently, each according to the evangelists' distinctive emphases. Whatever their differences, however, common to all four evangelists is the conviction that Jesus performed healings.

Is such a belief credible? Whether Jesus healed, or performed other kinds of miracles, raises the much larger questions of the credibility of miracles generally and why we believe some things to be true and not others. Though members of the Flat Earth Society may dispute that the earth is spherical, pictures from space confirm for most persons that it is. Those pictures are what some scholars call "warrants," the reasons under-girding what we believe to be true and that we cite if questioned about those beliefs. In the case of the shape of the earth, the warrants provide certainty – they are "tight." We bring tight warrants also to a story such as that of Elisha's causing an ax head to float to the surface by throwing a stick in after it (2 Kings 6:1–7): we can try the experiment on our own, and the physics of specific gravities of iron and water will provide quantified reasons why the experiment fails. It remains to be seen whether research in psychokinesis (roughly, "mind moving matter") will loosen such warrants (see the Broughton book cited in the reading list at the end of this volume).

When it comes to the body and illness and the treatment of illness, warrants are typically fairly loose. Startling remissions of usually fatal illnesses occur, as both patients and physicians attest. "Miracle" and "miraculous" are words commonly employed in such cases. Startling, "miraculous," indeed – but on reflection perhaps not so surprising. Bacteria and viruses are complex, often eluding diagnosis and capable of resisting or subverting medication directed at them, making diagnosis and especially prognosis difficult. A study in the *Journal of the*

American Medical Association recently reported, for example, that 80 per cent of 788 patients diagnosed with Lyme disease were in fact misdiagnosed. Various surveys have shown that about half the time a firm diagnosis of illnesses is not possible. Moreover, high-tech diagnostic tests may give false-positive and false-negative readings.

Also complicating the physician's task, and rendering medicine an art as well as a science, are the persons the physician seeks to help: each one is distinct in individuality and wondrously complex in body and mind and the relation between the two. Medical research is now demonstrating anew how great a role patients' attitude and emotions play in illness and healing.

The sick as self-healers

Over fifty years ago Walter B. Cannon, a neurologist and physiologist at the Harvard Medical School, investigated reports of a phenomenon known among anthropologists as "voodoo death" in which a person who has been put under a curse actually dies a short time later. Cannon helps us understand why by quoting at length an anthropologist's graphic account of how an Australian aboriginal reacts when he is cursed by having a bone pointed at him:

He stands aghast, with his eyes staring at the treacherous pointer, and with his hands lifted as though to ward off the lethal medium, which he imagines is pouring into his body. His cheeks blanch and his eyes become glassy and the expression of his face becomes horribly distorted . . . He attempts to shriek but usually the sound chokes in his throat, and all that one might see is froth at his mouth. His body begins to tremble and the muscles twist involuntarily. He sways backward and falls to the ground, and after a short time appears to be in a swoon; but soon after he writhes as if in mortal agony, and, covering his face with his hands, begins to moan. After a while he becomes very composed and crawls to his wurley [hut].

In "a comparatively short time" the man is dead.

The normal reactions to fear or rage are "fight or flight." Victims of the curse do neither for they are convinced, along with their social group, that nothing can avert their imminent death. The fear that would normally work for them, arousing their sympathico-adrenal system to prepare the heart, liver, and blood vessels for action, now work against them: the prolonged stress and excitation debilitates the body. Since victims are certain they are going to die, they refuse food and drink, thus contributing to further deterioration of their bodily functions. This certainty is reinforced by those around them, who withdraw and send the sufferers on their way to the world of the dead with rites of mourning. Medical intervention is to no avail. However, if a qualified member of the community performs rites to undo the curse, the victim soon recovers.

Such scenes from so-called primitive peoples may well seem remote from the modern Western world. Yet, thanks to the work especially of Hans Selye, most of us have become aware of how seriously stress can affect bodily functions. Earlier, during the two World Wars, accounts of soldiers who suffered disability or died from emotional shock, no life-threatening injuries being present, suggested that what one might call "psychic deaths" are perhaps not so far removed from our own reality. We all have doubtless known or heard of persons who sicken and die a few days after the death of a spouse; or, conversely, of persons on the verge of dying who seem to delay their deaths until after a loved one coming from afar arrives at their bedside. The branch of medicine that studies such phenomena is called psychoneuroimmunology, the study of the interactions between the nervous, endocrine, and immune systems, or, in more everyday language, between mind and body. In his book *Head First* (1989), Norman Cousins, who was invited as a lay person to join the medical faculty of the University of California at Los Angeles, provides an accessible account of research in this relatively new area of study.

Cousins cites numerous examples (what is called anecdotal evidence) of how attitudes and emotions affect health and healing, both positively and negatively. Persons who have received bad news from their doctors will bring some understanding to Cousins' reports of two young men who each, upon hearing they had been diagnosed with multiple sclerosis, immediately experienced severe intensification of their symptoms. A woman told she had a non-functioning kidney went suddenly deaf.

Much of Cousins' book is devoted to reports of experiments that go beyond such anecdotal evidence to demonstrate, biologically and physiologically, the close relation between mind and body, for example:

> Cancer patients who experience the nausea and other common reactions to chemotherapy before actually receiving the treatment.
>
> Cancer patients who are told their chemotherapy will cause hair loss and then do indeed lose their hair even though they receive only placebos (pills with no medication).
>
> The effects of depression on the immune system.
>
> The panic that constricts blood vessels, causing death in the first twenty-four hours after a heart attack.

Cousins subtitles his book *The Biology of Hope and the Healing Power of the Human Spirit*. This is the other, positive side of the relation between body and mind: hope, the will to live, laughter, purpose can contribute significantly to healing. Making an effort to live even in the face of death enhances life both for the sick person and those around her or him. Part of Cousins' assignment was to work with depressed and distraught patients referred to him by physicians who hoped that sessions with Cousins could create a more positive environment for the conventional medical care the patients were receiving. The results, for patients and their family and their physician, were encouraging, sometimes remarkable, though most were not as dramatic as the case of the young woman whose malignant breast tumor the size of a hand grenade disappeared within a week after seeing Cousins and having had her hope restored through learning about her own resources for fighting the disease.

These anecdotal and biological evidences of the human capacity for healing are put in wider perspective by the judgment of Dr. Franz Ingelfinger, late editor of the prestigious *New England Journal of Medicine*, that 85 percent of illnesses fall within the body's power to heal. That power is not exercised in isolation, however. The sick person's physician, family, and larger social group also play significant roles. There is, moreover, a long tradition of healers. Jesus stands in this tradition.

Jesus as healer

Modern anthropological studies of healers in various indigenous cultures bring out several elements common to most of them. One is that ritual procedures, involving gestures, material means, and utterances, are customary. Another is that healers enjoy a recognized status comparable, one might say, to that accorded physicians and psychiatrists in modern Western society. Moreover, the healer's social group is convinced that healings occur through the efforts of healers, with failures being explained in various ways. There is, thus, as Freud once observed, a "condition of 'expectant' faith" that healing is possible.

Even a healer who is skeptical or doubtful of the possibility of healings may still be able to heal if his or her social group believes in healings and the healer's powers. This is evident from a revealing autobiography of a Kwakiutl healer in British

Columbia published by anthropologist Franz Boas in 1930. Before becoming a healer he was skeptical of cures by healers among his people, and he determined to expose them as frauds. In order to learn their techniques, however, he had to associate with them, which led to his being identified as a healer himself, with persons coming to him for healing. He acquired a formidable reputation as a healer, but continued to doubt healers' powers, and was ambivalent about his own. As anthropologist Claude Lévi-Strauss comments, the man became a great healer not because he healed but because he had acquired a reputation as a great healer. His was a social and cultural setting in which healings were expected, and he fulfilled those expectations in carrying out the healing rituals he remained doubtful about.

As we have seen in earlier chapters, the world of Jesus' day was similar. Persons who doubted the possibility of healings were the exception. The New Testament evangelists' reports that the sick came or were brought to Jesus for healing are therefore not unlikely. And in view of the considerations about healing outlined in the preceding paragraphs, healings would, by present-day critical criteria, seem the most plausible of the miracles ascribed to Jesus.

Plausibility is the best one can hope for, however, for, as was pointed out earlier, the distance in time from the healings recorded in the gospels preclude the possibility of direct investigation and positive proof of healing. The gospels are themselves removed several decades from the events they record and are imbued with a different sense of history and science from our own. The aspect of the healings that is perhaps most difficult for a present-day historian to assess is the suddenness of the healings reported. Such are not impossible, contends Morton Smith, a very critical reader of the gospel records, if one invokes the concept of "hysterical" illnesses which may produce fever, blindness, paralysis, and

other debilitating symptoms that could conceivably respond
quickly to an imposing personality with a reputation for
healing.

The "common-sense" notion that physicians can promote –
or hinder – healing simply by their attitude toward their
patients has been demonstrated numerous times by medical
researchers in our day. That certain persons have the gift of
healing, such as is ascribed to Jesus, has also been the subject
of research in recent years. Some of this research is described
in non-technical language in Tom Harpur's recent book *The
Uncommon Touch: An Investigation of Spiritual Healing*
(1994). Such healing has received significant recognition in
British medicine; healers are now on the staff of some hospi-
tals, there are a number of doctor-healer teams, and some
British doctors now refer patients to healers. Touch, or the
technique of near touch, often figures in their healings, as it
sometimes does in the gospels' accounts of Jesus' healings (see
chapter 2 above). More than touch is involved, however.

As is indicated by the adjective "spiritual" in Harpur's
subtitle, the healers he profiles commonly concern themselves
with more than the physical symptoms of the persons who
come to them. The whole person is involved in illness and
healing, as the research on which Cousin reports also makes
clear. It is recognized also in the story of Jesus' healing of the
paralyzed man discussed in chapter 2 above: Jesus first tells the
man his sins are forgiven (Mark 2:7).

That statement, interestingly, follows upon the observation
that "Jesus saw *their* faith" – that is, the faith of the people
who went to the trouble of gaining access to Jesus by digging
through the roof of a house. In some early Christian accounts
of healing by Jesus' followers, the role of the sick person's
social group is significant. The Letter of James (5:14–16)
advises members of the community who fall sick to "call for
the elders of the church," who are to "pray over them" and

anoint them "with oil in the name of the Lord." Oil as a medication was commonly used in treating sickness or injury (see Mark 6:13; Luke 10:34). Here in James, however, more is involved. The oil is connected with "the name of the Lord" and with prayer, and it is the elders, representing the church, who carry out the rite of healing. The result, continues the author, is that the prayer will heal the sick persons and "the Lord will raise them up" from their sickbeds. Moreover, any sins they have committed "will be forgiven." Near the end of the second century CE Irenaeus, bishop of Lyons (France), reported that resurrections were performed when the whole church in a particular area assembled, fasted, and prayed (*Against Heresies* 2.31.2). Whether the "dead" were actually dead, and were actually resurrected, is impossible to say at this remove. These passages, however, point to the importance the early followers of Jesus attached to the role of the community in healing – a point that hardly needs stressing in our day when "supportive community" and "support group" have become part of everyday discourse.

Restoring to community those isolated from it by sickness is, as we saw in earlier chapters, one of the marks of Jesus' healings as recorded in the New Testament gospels. Some recent research suggests that in some cases sick persons may not wish to be reintegrated into their communities, that their sickness expresses alienation from society and world. Perceiving the world as sick, and frustrated by efforts to heal it, their reaction is to become sick themselves, their individual sickness expressing – indeed, embodying, as it were – a wider sickness. One of the fundamental elements in the gospels' portraits of Jesus, most likely based on the historical Jesus, is his concern not only about individual illnesses but social illnesses as well.

His healings on the Sabbath, for example, take place, say the gospels, in the face of opposition from religious leaders who, in

their understandable concern for religious identity marked by
sabbath-keeping, lose sight of compassion. Moreover, according to the gospels, compassion was for Jesus not something
you put a price on: unlike various similar figures in his day,
Jesus charged no fee for his healings. Even as God fed the birds
of the air and clothed the lilies of the field (Matt. 6:25–33) and
caused the sun to shine and rain to fall on just and unjust alike
(5:45), so God's gift of healing was gratis. Jesus' calls to
discipleship (the subject of another book in this series[1]) were
invitations to others to live in a way that would demonstrate
God's compassion and care, also to those outside Jesus' immediate following. The Good Samaritan in the well-known
parable (Luke 10:29–37) exemplifies this: he crosses social
boundaries in order to tend the injured man's wounds and then
even to provide care during his period of recuperation. The
Samaritan thus makes up for the neglect of the man's own
compatriots.

That Jesus' followers did in fact follow in the Good Samaritan's footsteps is attested not only by early Christian sources
but, more significantly, by outsiders. Galen, the noted second-
century pagan philosopher and physician, observed that Christians, without benefit of philosophy, led the kind of moral
lives advocated by philosophers. Julian, the Roman emperor
who rejected the Christianity in which he was raised and
during his brief reign (361–63 CE) tried to revive a declining
paganism, saw as crucial to any such revival the imitation of
Christians in their concern for those in need, including pagans
(Julian, *Letter* 22, Loeb edition). The Christian hostels for
strangers to which Julian calls attention were among the many
such institutions that, then and subsequently, owed their
founding in part to the example of Jesus, the compassionate
healer of the New Testament gospels.

---

[1] James J. G. Dunn, *Jesus' Call to Discipleship* (1992).

Whether or not the accounts of Jesus' healings can be pronounced "historical" by current scholarship, the New Testament portraits of Jesus as healer have inspired and given hope to countless readers and hearers of the gospels. Readers of the gospels are also well aware, however, that Jesus did not heal all the sick people in the world. His healings are presented in the gospels not as panacea – the end of all pain and suffering – but as signs – glimpses – of the reign of God that Jesus proclaims. His first followers interpreted that reign as an imminent, splendiferous future presided over by Jesus, with themselves alongside in positions of power. That, as we have seen, turns out to be a mistaken notion, rejected by the Jesus of the gospels and dispelled by the picture of the powerful healer hanging powerless on a cross.

One of the New Testament resurrection stories depicts the risen Jesus as healing the pain and confusion his crucifixion has caused two of his followers by reframing their perception of that event (Luke 24:13–35). The two are on their way from Jerusalem to a nearby village named Emmaus. They fail to recognize Jesus when he joins them. After inquiring the reason for their sad faces, he explains that the tragic and seemingly senseless end of Jesus was in fact God's plan, attested in the scriptures. When they invite him to join them at their evening meal, he breaks the bread and gives some to each. This familiar action opens their eyes to the true identity of this stranger. He then vanishes.

As he is changed, so too are they as they see his death in a new light. His crucifixion and resurrection are now seen as the conclusive victory over the sickness and death that stand in contradiction to God's reign. As the Messiah must first suffer and only "then enter into his glory" (Luke 24:26), so too it will be for his followers. As disciples are not above their teacher (Matt. 10:24//Luke 6:40, "Q"; cf. John 13:16), so they can expect to suffer as he did (John 15:20). The glorious future

Jesus' followers once envisaged remained future, a "not yet." For the present, what the Jesus of the gospels called each of them to was to follow him in sharing the pain and suffering of the world – to become, like him, a wounded healer.

Questions for further thought and discussion

1 Jesus as Healer· Prologue

1. What is "health"? "sickness"? "healing"?
2. What roles are played in healing by physicians and other health care workers? By relatives and friends of the sick person? By the sick person?
3. What differences do you see between attitudes to sickness, health, and healing in Jesus' day and today? In the treatment of sickness then and today? Why the differences? What are the pros and cons of the differences?
4. Have you ever turned to "alternative medicine" for help, or do you know persons who have? What were the reasons – and the results?
5. What is your experience with "home remedies"? How do they compare with home remedies in Jesus' day?
6. What is your perception of medical treatment of women as compared to that of men?

2 Jesus as Healer: The Gospel of Mark

1. What are the similarities and differences between "leprosy" today and the "leprosy" referred to in the New Testament, or in the Bible generally (cf. Lev. 12, 14; Num. 12:15; 2 Kings 5 and 7:3–4) and in the attitudes to persons afflicted with it?
2. Compare and contrast biblical reports of "possession by demons" and modern diagnoses of "mental illnesses' and attitudes to such afflictions then and now.

3. What comparisons and contrasts do you see in belief in the power of words and names in Jesus' day and today? How are "words" used in treating mental illness today?

4. How were material means used by healers in Jesus' day? How are they used in treating mental illness today?

5. How important is "touch" in healing? In life generally?

6. What connection – if any – do you see between sickness and "sin"?

7. If you had been living in Jesus' day, do you think you might have been found among his supporters or his opponents?

8. How do power and powerlessness figure into the story of Jesus in Mark? Do you see any implications for today?

9. Does the question of Jesus in Mark (and other New Testament gospels), "Who do you say that I am?," seem important (and challenging), or remote and antiquarian, today?

3 Jesus as Healer: The Gospel of Matthew

1. What features of the Matthean portrait of Jesus as healer set him apart from the Markan portrait as well as from other healers of the time – or today? What do they have in common?

2. What effect does the terseness of most of the healing accounts in Matthew as compared with Mark have on you as reader?

3. How do the Matthean themes of discipleship, faith/little faith, and teaching figure into some of the healing accounts?

4. How do Matthew 23 and 25:35–40 relate to healing – or do they?

5. If you had to choose between the Markan and Matthean portraits of Jesus as healer, which would you choose, and why?

4 Jesus as Healer: The Gospel of Luke

1. How do the healing stories in the Gospel of Luke contribute to the "assurance" the author promises Theophilus? Do they "assure" you?
2. What do the connections between Jesus and Elijah and Elisha in Luke contribute to the author's portrait of Jesus as healer?
3. How do the healing stories and Jesus' reaching out to the marginalized, and how do the various role reversals in the Lukan travel narrative (9:51–18:14), relate to the healing of society? to Jesus' passion and death?
4. How might Luke 24:13–25 be seen as a healing story?
5. Among the three portraits of Jesus as healer in Mark, Matthew, and Luke, which would you choose, and why?

5 Jesus as Healer: The Gospel of John

1. What are some of the basic differences between the healing accounts in the Gospel of John and those in the first three (Synoptic) gospels? How do the dialogues and discourses that follow the accounts relate to the accounts and what do they contribute to the picture of Jesus as healer?
2. What is the relation between seeing and believing in the healing stories in John and in this gospel generally? What is your own view of "seeing" and "believing"?
3. What role do you think that "wanting to be well" (John 5:14) plays in healing – or in health generally?
4. What kinds of healing and what kinds of "life" are portrayed and offered in this gospel? Do they "make sense" to you?
5. If you had to choose between the four gospel portraits of Jesus as healer, which would you choose, and why? How do the four complement one another?

6 Jesus as Healer: Apocryphal Writings

1. Some early Christians evidently found healing accounts like those in the apocryphal writings attractive. What is your reaction to them? Do you see any value in the accounts?
2. To the one New Testament story of Jesus' boyhood, which depicts him as precocious and standing in a special relationship with his "Father" (Luke 2:41–52), early Christians added others portraying him as a remarkable, wondrous child, as in the *Infancy Gospel of Thomas*. Can you think of modern examples where stories came to be told of the unusual or wondrous childhoods of later-to-be famous persons, whether historical or fictional?

7 "In His Name": Jesus Heals Through His Followers

1. How does the picture of Paul as healer in the Acts of the Apostles compare with what he says about himself in his letters? Which do you find more sympathetic?
2. How do the healing accounts in Acts compare with those in the four gospels?
3. For the author of Acts why is calling out the name of Jesus, or reciting a formula using his name, insufficient to perform healings? What might be some implications for healing today?
4. How would you assess claims – ancient or modern – that one person is a magician and another a healer?

8 Did Jesus Really Heal?

1. What are "warrants"? Why are some "tight" and others "loose"? How does that bear on the credibility of healing accounts, or on healing itself?

2. What factors do you see as entering into healing (or sickness and health)?
3. Can you suggest reasons why "Jesus as healer" played, and continues to play, an important role in society and culture?

Suggestions for further reading

Ancient sources

Various annotated editions of modern translations of the Bible are available, including the following editions of the New Revised Standard Version (the translation cited in this book):

Meeks, Wayne, general editor, with Jouette Bassler, Werner Lemke, Susan Niditch, and Eileen Schuller, 1993. *The Harper Collins Study Bible: New Revised Standard Version with Apocryphal/Deuterocanonical Books*. London and New York: Harper Collins.

Metzger, Bruce M., and Roland E. Murphy, eds., 1991. *The New Oxford Annotated Bible with the Apocryphal/Deutero-canonical Books*. New York: Oxford University Press.

Authors and books referred to in this volume that are not in the Bible may be found in the following books and series:

Charlesworth, James H. ed., 1983, 1985. *The Old Testament Pseudepigrapha*. 2 vols. Garden City, NY: Doubleday. Translations (with detailed commentary) of early Jewish and Christian writings that were not included in the Bible.

Vermes, Geza, trans. and ed., 1987. *The Dead Sea Scrolls in English*. 3rd, rev. ed. London et al.: Penguin Books. Translations and interpretations.

Schneemelcher, Wilhelm, and Edgar Hennecke, eds., 1991–92. *New Testament Apocrypha*. 2 vols. English trans. edited by R. McL. Wilson. 2nd, rev. ed. Cambridge, England: James Clarke. Translations (with helpful interpretations) of early Christian writings that were not included in the New Testament.

Roberts, Alexander, and James Donaldson, eds., 1884–86. *The Ante-Nicene Fathers*. 10 vols. Reprinted, Grand Rapids, MI: Eerdmans. Old but readily accessible translations of early Christian writings of the first three centuries.

Robinson, James M., General Editor, 1988. *The Nag Hammadi Library in English*. 3rd, rev. ed. San Francisco et al.: Harper and Row. Translations (with helpful interpretations of the Coptic papyri found at Nag Hammadi in Egypt in 1945 and now known as the Coptic Gnostic Library.

The Loeb Classical Library. English translations of Greek and Latin authors; the Greek and Latin texts are provided as well. Included are Jewish authors cited in this volume whose works are in Greek, Philo of Alexander and Josephus. Cambridge, MA: Harvard University Press and London: Heinemann.

Clendenning, Logan, ed., 1960. *Source Book of Medical History*. New York: Dover. Egyptian, Greek, Roman, and subsequent sources.

Edelstein, Emma J., and Ludwig, 1945. *Asclepius: A Collection and Interpretation of the Testimonies*. 2 vols. Baltimore: Johns Hopkins University Press. Translations of the many ancient texts concerning healings attributed to the god Asclepius (vol. 1) together with a detailed examination of the texts (vol. 2).

LiDonnici, Lynn R., 1995. *The Epidaurian Miracle Inscriptions: Text, Translation and Commentary*. Atlanta: Scholars Press. A recent edition of the Asclepius healing texts from Epidauros.

Betz, Hans Dieter, ed., 1992. *The Greek Magical Papyri in Translation Including the Demotic Spells.* 2nd ed. Chicago and London: University of Chicago Press. The introduction and footnotes to the translations facilitate understanding.

Meyer, Marvin, and Richard Smith, eds., 1994. *Ancient Christian Magic: Coptic Texts of Ritual Power.* San Francisco: HarperSanFrancisco. Though only Coptic texts are specified in the title, translations of Greek texts are included as well (chap. 2). Includes explanatory introductions and footnotes.

Gager, John G., 1992. *Curse Tablets and Binding Spells from the Ancient World.* New York and Oxford: Oxford University Press. Translations with explanatory introductions and footnotes.

Modern sources

General

The following reference volumes have articles on subjects such as "disease," "leprosy," "demons," "physicians," "medicine and healing," "miracle," "magic," as well as individuals named in this book; they also contain suggestions for further reading:

Achtemeier, Paul J., General Ed.; Roger S. Boraas, Michael Fishbane, Pheme Perkins, William O. Walker, Jr., assoc. eds., 1985. *Harper's Bible Dictionary.* San Francisco et al.: Harper and Row.

Freedman, David Noel, Editor-in-Chief; Gary A. Herion, David F. Graf, John David Pleins, Assoc. Eds.; Astrid B. Beck, managing ed., 1992. *Anchor Bible Dictionary.* 6 vols. New York: Doubleday.

Cross, F. L., and E. A. Livingstone, eds., 1974. *The Oxford Dictionary of the Christian Church.* 2nd, rev. ed. London and New York: Oxford University Press.

Ferguson, Everett, Editor, and Michael P. McHugh, Frederick
Norris, Assoc. Eds., David M. Scholer, consulting ed., 1990.
Encyclopedia of Early Christianity. New York and London:
Garland. (A second edition is forthcoming.)

Hammond, N. G. L., and H. H. Scullard, eds., 1970. *The
Oxford Classical Dictionary*. 2nd, rev. ed. Oxford:
Clarendon Press.

1 Jesus as Healer: Prologue

Scarborough, John, 1969. *Roman Medicine*. Ithaca: Cornell
University Press.

Jackson, Ralph, 1988. *Doctors and Diseases in the Roman
Empire*. Norman, OK and London: University of Oklahoma
Press. Includes chapters on fitness, food, hygiene, physicians, gynecology, birth, contraception, surgery, the army,
gods, dying, death, and a helpful bibliography of related
works.

Kee, Howard Clark, 1986. *Medicine, Miracle, and Magic in
New Testament Times*. Cambridge, England and New
York: Cambridge University Press.

Demand, Nancy, 1994. *Birth, Death and Motherhood in Classical Greece*. Baltimore: Johns Hopkins University Press.

Hanson, Ann Ellis, 1991. "Continuity and Change: Three Case
Studies in Hippocratic Gynecological Therapy and
Theory." In Sarah B. Pomeroy, ed., *Women's History and
Ancient History*. Pp. 73–109. Chapel Hill: North Carolina
University Press. Included in this examination of ancient
gynecological theory and practice is discussion of how
these relate to "home remedies."

Tolstoy, Leo, 1981. *The Death of Ivan Ilyich*. Trans. by Lynn
Solotaroff. Tolstoy's novella of 1885 raises questions about
"health," "sickness," "healing," and whether death can be
healing. Toronto et al.: Bantam Books.

2–5 Jesus as Healer: The Gospels of Mark, Matthew, Luke, John

Easy comparison of the New Testament gospels with one another is made possible by "Synopses," which display the gospel texts alongside one another in parallel columns or (horizontal) rows of type:

Throckmorton, Burton H., ed., 1979. *Gospel Parallels: A Synopsis of the First Three Gospels with Alternative Readings from the Manuscripts and Non-canonical Parallels.* 4th, rev. ed. Nashville: Thomas Nelson. An English version of the Greek *Synopsis* by Albert Huck and Hans Lietzmann.

Aland, Kurt, ed., 1970. *Synopsis of the Four Gospels: Greek-English Edition of the Synopsis Quattuor Evangeliorum with the Text of the Revised Standard Version.* Stuttgart: United Bible Societies.

Beare, Francis Wright, 1962. *The Earliest Records of Jesus: A Companion to* Synopsis of the First Three Gospels *by Albert Huck.* New York and Nashville: Abingdon Press. Useful commentary on each section of gospel texts in the Huck-Lietzmann/Throckmorton Synopses.

The following provide introductions to current scholarly views on "Q," on the formation of the New Testament gospels, on each of the gospels generally, and on various topics mentioned in chapters 2–5 of the present volume:

Kee, Howard Clark, 1990. *What Can We Know about Jesus?* Cambridge, England: Cambridge University Press.

1993. *Understanding the New Testament.* 5th, rev. ed. Englewood Cliffs, NJ: Prentice-Hall. See Part II and pp. 391–93 (contents of Q).

Spivey, Robert A., and D. Moody Smith, 1995. *Anatomy of the New Testament: A Guide to Its Structure and Meaning.* 5th, rev. ed. Englewood Cliffs, NJ: Prentice-Hall. See Part 1.

Mack, Burton L., 1993. *The Lost Gospel: The Book of Q & Christian Origins.* San Francisco: HarperSanFrancisco. Chapter 5 offers a translation of the contents of Q in its successive strata as these have been postulated by recent scholarly studies.

Cadbury, Henry J., 1920. *The Style and Literary Method of Luke.* Cambridge, MA: Harvard University Press. Reprinted, New York: Kraus, 1962. Discusses (pp. 39–72) "The Alleged Medical Language of Luke" and related topics.

    1937. *The Peril of Modernizing Jesus.* Reprinted, London: SPCK, 1955.

The articles on these subjects in the Bible dictionaries cited above are also illuminating. They also provide references to recent studies and commentaries on each of the gospels.

On the "Messianic Secret":

Perrin, Norman, 1976. "Secret, Messianic." In Keith Crim, General Ed., and Lloyd Bailey, Sr., Victor Furnish, Emory Buck, eds., *The Interpreter's Dictionary of the Bible*: Supplementary Volume. Pp. 798–99.

Classic anthropological studies that bear on the relation between individual bodies and social bodies:

Evans-Pritchard, E. E., 1937. *Witchcraft, Oracles and Magic Among the Azande.* Oxford: Clarendon Press.

Douglas, Mary, 1966. *Purity and Danger: An Analysis of*

Concepts of Pollution and Taboo. Harmondsworth et al.: Penguin.

On the "wounded healer":

Nouwen, Henri J. M., 1972. *The Wounded Healer: Ministry in Contemporary Society.* Garden City, NY: Doubleday.

6 Jesus as Healer: Apocryphal Writings

English translations of the apocryphal writings referred to in this chapter will be found in the Hennecke-Schneemelcher volumes cited above under "Ancient Sources."

7 Jesus as Healer: Jesus Heals Through His Followers

The Ante-Nicene Fathers cited above provide old but accessible English translations of Justin Martyr, Irenaeus, Celsus (in Origen, *Against Celsus*) and Tertullian. An English translation of the *Acts of Thomas* will be found in the Hennecke-Schneemelcher volumes.

Articles, including references to recent studies and commentaries, on the Acts of the Apostles will be found in the Bible dictionaries cited above. *The Anchor Bible Dictionary* has an article on the *Acts of Thomas*.

MacMullen, Ramsay, 1984. *Christianizing the Roman Empire (AD 100–400).* New Haven and London: Yale University Press. Argues for the importance of Christian healings in spreading Christianity. Extensive bibliography.
Vonhoff, Heinz, 1971. *People Who Care: An Illustrated*

History of Human Compassion. Philadelphia: Fortress Press. A survey from pre-Christian to modern times.

Hanawalt, Emily Albu, and Carter Lindberg, eds , 1994. *Through the Eye of a Needle: Judeo-Christian Roots of Social Welfare.* Kirksville, MO: Thomas Jefferson University Press. More recent than Vonhoff, the chapters by well-known scholars look at social welfare in ancient Judaism and the Near East, the New Testament, ancient Eastern Christianity (including the work of Byzantine women), the medieval period, and the sixteenth-century Reformations.

Remus, Harold, 1983. *Pagan-Christian Conflict Over Miracle in the Second Century.* Cambridge, MA: Philadelphia Patristic Foundation. Examination of the social and cultural settings of such conflicts.

1992. "Miracle: New Testament." In *Anchor Bible Dictionary* 4:856–69. A similar examination of "miracle."

1990. "Miracle." In *Encyclopedia of Early Christianity*, pp. 600–04. Extends the examination on into late antiquity.

8 Did Jesus Really Heal?

Cannon, W. B., 1942. "'Voodoo Death.'" *American Anthropologist* 44:169–81. Reprinted in *Psychosomatic Medicine* 19 (1957):182–90 and (abridged) in W. Lessa and E. Z. Vogt, eds., *Reader in Comparative Religion: An Anthropological Approach* (3rd ed.; New York: Harper and Row, 1972). A physiological explanation of how a curse can kill under certain conditions.

Lévi-Strauss, Claude, 1967. *Structural Anthropology.* Trans. by C. Jacobson and B. G. Schoepf. Garden City, NY: Doubleday Anchor Books. Contains an account of a young Kwakiutl man who, setting out to expose healers, himself acquired a great reputation as a healer.

Selye, Hans, 1956. *The Stress of Life.* New York et al.:

McGraw-Hill. "The main purpose of this book is to tell, in a generally understandable language, what medicine has learned about stress" (p. vii).

Siirala, Aarne, 1964. *The Voice of Illness: A Study in Therapy and Prophecy*. Introduction by Gotthard Booth. Philadelphia: Fortress Press. Illness as an expression of social ill, and the role of words in sickness and healing.

Cousins, Norman, 1989. *Head First: The Biology of Hope and the Healing Power of the Human Spirit*. London et al.: Penguin Books. Cousins' report of anecdotal and physiological evidence of the close relation between mind and body in healing. Bibliography of popular and technical writings.

Moyers, Bill, 1993. *Healing and the Mind*. New York: Doubleday. Interviews with various physicians and other specialists, based on the television series on the Public Broadcasting System.

Harpur, Tom, 1994. *The Uncommon Touch: An Investigation of Spiritual Healing*. Toronto: McClelland and Stewart. A sympathetic but sober study of modern healers and their healings.

Broughton, Richard S., 1991. *Parapsychology: The Controversial Science*. New York: Ballantine Books. Includes a chapter on research in psychokinesis.

Smith, Morton, 1978. *Jesus the Magician*. San Francisco et al.: Harper and Row. Adduces many parallels from so-called magical texts, to argue that Jesus was a "magician."

Garrett, Susan, 1989. "Light on a Dark Subject and Vice Versa: Magic and Magician in the New Testament." In Jacob Neusner et al., eds., *Religion, Science, and Magic in Concert and Conflict*. New York and Oxford: Oxford University Press. Includes a critical assessment of Smith's book.

Faraone, Christopher A., and Dirk Obbink, eds., 1991. *Magika Hiera: Ancient Greek Magic and Religion*. New York and

Oxford: Oxford University Press. Recent scholarship on various aspects of the relation between "magic" and "religion"; bibliography.

Crossan, John Dominic, 1991. *The Historical Jesus: The Life of a Mediterranean Peasant*. San Francisco: Harper Collins. Includes discussions of Jesus as healer. Extensive bibliography.

Sanders, E. P., 1996. *The Historical Figure of Jesus*. Toronto: Penguin. A more recent discussion, from another scholarly standpoint.

Index of Subjects and Names

Index of Ancient Writings

Old Testament Apocrypha and Pseudepigrapha

Dead Sea Scrolls

Josephus